In th  House of Ideas

Conversation, Influence, and Persuasion

by Bill Gladwell

Second Edition

In the House of Ideas... Conversation, Influence, and Persuasion

**In the House of Ideas... Conversation, Influence, and
Persuasion**

For information contact...

Bill Gladwell

(702) 721-8456

HypnosisForHumans.com
Bill@HypnosisForHumans.com

In the House of Ideas... Conversation, Influence, and Persuasion

"You cannot hypnotize someone against their will, but you can hypnotize someone without their knowledge."

—Bill Gladwell

Dedication

This book is dedicated to my beautiful wife, Summer. Without her, none of what I do would matter.

Table Of Contents

In the House of Ideas... Conversation, Influence, and Persuasion

About Bill Gladwell

Bill Gladwell is an Influence and Persuasion Expert.

For over 30 years, Bill Gladwell has been an author, entertainer, speaker, and consultant in the corporate world where he has helped hundreds of thousands of people develop and master strong social skills, easily meet others, and get more of what they want.

- Stop standing against the wall at networking events waiting on someone to talk to you as if it was an 8th-grade dance; learn to confidently walk up to anyone anywhere and open a conversation and command the room.
- Never again be in the position of not knowing what to say next; lead every conversation in the direction that you choose.
- Quit accepting wishy-washy words and promises; gain solid commitments for what happens next.
- Make "hoping" everything will turn out okay a thing of the past; know that you have the skills, tools, and ability to tip the outcome in your favor.

"Think 'How to Win Friends & Influence People' but updated, hipper, and more effective."

(That's a quote from a boot camp attendee, so take it up with her, Dale Carnegie fans!)

Bill is an expert in how people interact within a group. Individuals in a group are influenced by one another's behavior making them more predictable and suggestible, and Bill teaches you how to use this phenomenon to ethically persuade others.

(Remember, a group can be as small as just two people, so what Bill teaches applies to any human interaction that you have.)

People are your most valuable resource. When you learn to powerfully influence others in an ethical manner, you will get more of what you want. What Bill teaches can immediately be implemented in the real world to help you hear "yes" more often in less time.

To you, this may mean making more sales, increasing your income, moving up in your company, and effectively leading people. Others may want the power to affect their own behavior and change their relationships, their emotions, and the direction of their life.

Bill designs his consulting to condition you to effectively communicate with others, quickly build deep connections, be more influential and capable in your interactions, and powerfully persuade people.

Why Hire Bill?

Bill has more than 30 years of experience in his field of expertise.

Without knowing it, Bill began his career in 1988 as a junior in high school when he participated in a hypnosis experiment in psychology class. He spent the following weekend in the library studying every book about hypnosis that was on the shelf taking notes that filled three large binders. With this new-found knowledge, Bill set out to hypnotize any of his classmates who agreed to be a guinea pig. With a few successful attempts at hypnotizing others, Bill was hooked.

Upon graduation in 1989 and while earning his BBA degree, Bill got the opportunity to attend a weekend seminar conducted by Tony Robbins at which he met the people who would put him on the fast track to becoming who he is today.

Bill received his first certification in Neuro-Linguistic Programming™ (NLP™) from Richard Bandler and The Society of Neuro-Linguistic Programming™; and shortly after, he became a certified hypnotherapist from The American School of Hypnotherapy.

Bill became a trainer for The Society of Applied Hypnosis and focused on consulting with counselors, social workers, and marriage and family therapist helping them learn and integrate hypnosis into their practices. Bill's courses allowed these professionals to earn continuing education units while adding a new dimension to their current offerings.

Bill also earned expert level certifications in Micro Expressions Training and Subtle Expressions Training from the Paul Eckman Group, LLC.

With a background in the medical community, Bill was courted by the pharmaceutical industry to consult on ethical sales, persuasion, and influence techniques. Bill worked with ALZA Pharmaceuticals, Inc.; Indevus Pharmaceuticals, Inc.; Innovex; Janssen Pharmaceutica, Inc.; Johnson & Johnson; Odyssey Pharmaceuticals, Inc.; Ortho-McNeil Pharmaceutical; and Quintiles.

Bill now consults with organizations across the United States teaching them how to master and implement ethical influence and persuasion skills into their existing infrastructure.

Entertaining, Interactive, and Unforgettable

As if the influence and persuasion skills that Bill teaches during his keynotes and seminars are not enough by themselves, Bill is a seasoned and critically-acclaimed entertainer. Bill had the #1 rated show out of 60+ shows in the Gatlinburg and Pigeon Forge, Tennessee region for many years; the #1 nightlife on Hilton Head Island; and the #1 performance across the United States as rated by the VIP guests of Diamond Resorts. (For comparison, Céline Dion was #2.)

While gaining skills that they can immediately implement in the real world, Bill brings people on stage, makes the learning experience fun, and creates moments that will be talked about for a very long time. In other words, Bill helps make your event unforgettable.

It's all about you!

Every business is different, and so many speakers and consultants attempt to push their clients through the same hole. Bill conducts extensive research into your organization, studies your mission, values, goals, and your ultimate outcome for your event. Bill takes this information and builds a program specifically relevant to your organization with the most current data on influence and persuasion.

Support

Studies have shown that 77% of learning is forgotten in just 6 days if not reinforced.

When Bill steps off the stage, he is not done yet. Bill offers support via email, telephone, and video conferencing after your event to answer any questions that may emerge as your team implements their new skills in the real world. Live sessions are also available to your team to ensure that they remember, internalize, and utilize what they have learned. Additionally, continuing education is available with the most up-to-date studies, skills, and new developments in the field of influence and persuasion.

Bill believes that if you are not learning new things and growing, you are moving backward. You must stay at least one step ahead of your clients and your competition.

You should probably contact Bill right now.

(702) 721-8456
Bill@HypnosisForHumans.com

<u>Introduction</u>

You are reading my personal notes on conversation, influence, and persuasion that I use daily.

These pages will help you learn new skills and develop the attitude you must have to utilize these skills.

Throughout this book, I refer to "conversational hypnosis". I will explain what conversational hypnosis is in the upcoming pages. For now, just know that hypnosis is essentially purposeful communication; and conversational hypnosis is simply purposeful communication during any conversation you may have with another individual or even a group.

You will also notice that I use the term "subject" throughout this book. When I use the term "subject", I am referring to the person or persons with whom you are communicating.

Why would I teach conversational hypnosis, and why would you want to learn it?

I teach conversational hypnosis, because I do not expect the majority of the people who are reading this book to become hypnotherapists with offices and private clients. **Most of you simply want to learn to become more influential, lead people, and get more of what you want.**

- If you are an entertainer, you will have more impact.
- If you are a salesperson, you will raise your close ratio.
- If you are a speaker, you will become more inspirational.
- If you are a teacher, you will command more respect from your students.
- If you are a parent, your children will develop a new found respect for you.

Get the picture? If you are a "whatever", you will get better and more of it.

As you read this book, you will learn what hypnosis really is, and you will discover that you are already hypnotizing others every time you communicate. What I am teaching you is to communicate on purpose... with purpose.

The information you are about to master is broken down into individual lessons. Each chapter is a new lesson. With each lesson, I urge you to **use what you have learned <u>in the field (the real world)</u>**.

At the end of this introduction, you will find a link to a free hypnosis audio download designed to help you handle stress better. This is your first "field assignment". I want you to experience what "overt hypnosis" is first so you can distinguish it from conversational hypnosis. **Download the MP3, and**

listen to it before starting on the next chapter; then listen to it several days in a row.

As you read this book, it is very important that you use and practice what you learn. If you do not use what you learn in real life situations, you will never master the art and skills of conversation, influence, and persuasion.

It takes guts, but you have to do it to internalize the material and build beliefs and new experiences inside yourself. If you cannot find your confidence deep down inside, I can help you with that. You have to **speak up, and let me know**.

You may be thinking of **how** you will use the skills that you learn. I encourage you to let the sky be your limit. Use what you learn in every area of your life.

Entertainers, you will draw your audience in, make them believe, and create very real moments of magic.

If you are a **counselor**, **therapist**, **social worker**, **physician, psychologist**, et cetera... you may want to increase your effectiveness with your clients and patients.

If you are a **sales person**, perhaps you want to explode your sales.

Are you searching for "the one" to spend the rest of your life with? Simply apply what you learn to meeting and building lasting relationships with others.

Parents, have more influence over your children than the "role models" on television who are arrested on a regular basis.

Whoever you are and whatever you do, you can use these skills to be more influential, to develop your charisma, to lead people, and to get what you want.

The only way that I can continue doing what I do is if people like you stay intrigued, fascinated, and entranced.

I made a promise to myself from the very beginning to stay accessible, because every single person is important. I welcome your emails, feedback, comments, and definitely your praises, compliments, and sheer admiration.

To download your **FREE HYPNOSIS AUDIO PROGRAM**, go to this link... https://hypnosisforhumans.com/in-the-house-of-ideas-supplemental-material

Can you make someone do something against their will?

This is the most common question that I get asked by far, and I thought I should answer it before you read further. It is not always phrased as "Can you make someone do something against their will?". Sometimes the question comes in the form of "Can you make someone rob a bank?" or "Can you make my husband do the dishes?" or some other related question.

I was at lunch with a friend who had watched a video of me on the Internet. He wanted to know how to do what I did in the video. I gave him a brief lesson on the skills and techniques that are contained in this book.

He asked me, "Why doesn't everyone learn this stuff?"

So, here is what I explained to my friend...

You are learning to communicate with a person's unconscious mind without their conscious knowledge.

Forget all the misinformation that you hear in the <u>media</u> and from other people. **You are getting only half of the story.**

If you ask them, "Can you make someone do something against their will?" The answer that you will get is, "I cannot make anyone do anything against their will?"

This answer is technically correct. The thing they will not tell you, and probably do not even know, is my solution:

Influence them without their knowledge, and you can change their will!

When you step into your subject's unconscious mind, you can take control of their will and turn it in the direction that you want.

Let me give you an example...

I can walk up to someone in a bar and say, "I am

going to use hypnosis to get you to buy me a beer." From that moment on, my subject is in a defensive mode. He can stop listening, walk away, question every word that comes out of my mouth, and use his will to resist any kind of suggestion to buy me a beer that I throw his way.

If, however, I use conversational hypnosis without his knowledge by weaving precise hypnotic language and suggestions into what appears to be a normal conversation; I will have a beer in my hand within minutes... as well as a supply for the rest of the night, cab fare home, and another story I can use in a later boot camp.

Does this sound too good to be true?

It is not.

It is, however, a very well kept secret.

Herein lies the answer to the question of... "Why isn't everyone learning this stuff?"

Most people who have mastered conversational hypnosis tend not to tell others about it; so you will not find their techniques in mainstream books, articles, or anywhere else.

In addition to the secrets being so closely guarded, there are other obstacles that keep 99% of the public from becoming members of this elite group.

- It is difficult to find someone who is an expert on conversational hypnosis.
- If you do find an "expert on conversational hypnosis", how do you know if they are legitimate and ethical? I have met many "experts on conversational hypnosis" who I discovered were charlatans after just a few minutes of speaking with them.
- Is the person really an expert in conversational hypnosis, or did he simply read a couple of books and realized he could make some money off of people who did not know any better?
- Does the person have real-life experience using conversational hypnosis? As Malcolm Gladwell writes in his book *Outliers*, it takes approximately 10,000 hours of focus on a subject or task to become an expert. Hence, most "experts" in this field are not really experts.

I started at the very bottom in 1989, and I had the sheer luck of being in the right places at the right times. I studied with the best of the best in the field, and I still seek out the masters to continue learning.

I also had the guts (and still do) to approach complete strangers to practice what I had learned. My mentors helped me tweak my skills until they were perfect; and I have continued to develop, study, and improve on a consistent and never-ending journey.

Because I truly know how difficult it is to find someone to teach you conversational hypnosis, I am giving you a glimpse of what is possible and a chance to begin your personal journey with one of the masters.

Welcome to a whole new world! It is yours... Take it!

<u>Do you want to know what hypnosis really is with no airy-fairy gobbledygook?</u>

Did you listen to the audio program? If not, stop reading now; and listen to it!

If you did not get that program downloaded due to technical difficulties, contact me. I will help you through it.

Especially if you have never been formally hypnotized, then **you must experience hypnosis <u>on purpose</u>** so you can recognize what a trance feels like.

Do not get tied up with the word <u>trance</u>. **A trance is simply an "altered state".** What is an "altered state"?

When I use the word "state", I am referring to your "emotional state".

STATE = EMOTIONAL STATE

So, **a trance occurs when you <u>change</u> from whatever emotion you are currently experiencing to a different emotion**.

For example... When someone tells you a joke to cheer you up, and you laugh; you have switched from one emotional state to another. In this case, you went from being in a state of feeling "down" to a state of "laughter". The state of "laughter" would be your trance, because it is your altered state.

In the case of the hypnosis audio program that you downloaded, I help you get relaxed. So, as you listen to the program, you are switching from whatever state you are in to a state of relaxation. Relaxation is the trance in this situation.

Understand?

I know it is different than what you see on television or in the movies or even in other people's hypnosis books and trainings; but a trance is nothing more than what I just explained. It has nothing to do with rituals, magic, or any other kind of esoteric gobbledygook. (Although, these particular beliefs produce rapid trance as you will learn in later chapters.)

Ideally, have someone else listen to the audio program after you, and watch them. This will allow you to **begin to recognize a trance** in others. When experiencing formal hypnosis for the first time, most people tell me, "It just feels like I was sitting there listening to you talk. I don't feel any differently."

That is great! To be truly masterful, your subject must have the perception that every idea that they have is coming from inside them; and everything is perfectly natural.

In reality, you are directing their thoughts and influencing their behavior.

On average, <u>you are "experiencing hypnosis" four times each hour</u>.

Need some examples?...

- Have you ever been driving down the road, and suddenly you cannot remember how you got the last few miles?
- Have you ever had the experience of talking to someone, and you lose yourself in thought. Now, you have to say, "I'm sorry. What did you just say?"
- Have you ever had the experience of "time flying"?
- Have you ever been so in to a movie that you cried, laughed, or became anxious along with or for the characters on the screen?
- Have you ever been sitting at a stop light, watching it intently, even after the light turned green?

These are all examples of every day hypnosis.

Although the phenomenon has been around and used since man crawled out of a primordial soup, the term "hypnosis" was coined in the 1800s by a physician; because he thought his patients were going to sleep, and he could perform feats such as pain free operations.

Hypnosis comes from the Greek word "Hypnos"... meaning sleep.

In fact, you are far from being asleep.

Hypnosis really is the process that takes place in your mind when you change from one emotional state to another. That is it. Nothing more, nothing less.

When you enter a trance (that change from one emotional state to another), that process is hypnosis. Whenever this happens, you become more suggestible. For some people it lasts for a split second, and other people are suggestible for longer periods of time.

Suggestible means that you tend to accept and follow commands and ideas with little or no resistance.

Let's take the example from above of driving down the road and suddenly not remembering how you traveled the last few miles. That span of time that you do not recall traveling is the time that you were suggestible, and it is also the time that a skilled hypnotist has access to your unconscious to do some installation and reprogramming.

The reason that most hypnotists will take you to a state of relaxation is because it is comfortable, and people are willing to stay in that enjoyable emotional state for an extended period of time.

The mistake that most hypnotists make, however, is thinking that relaxation is the key to hypnosis. It is absolutely not.

The key to hypnosis, again, is the change from one emotional state to another.

Since relaxation is an emotional state and the hypnotist is continually giving suggestions to listen to the sound of his voice, to continue to relax, to drift off, to open your mind to new possibilities, to remain in your suggestible state, et cetera; the hypnotist does not have to think, because he is surely going to hit the "suggestible window" as you make the emotional change.

I want you to be able to recognize this emotional change (the trance) as well as the window of suggestibility so you can perform your installation and reprogramming with precision instead of on accident. That is what this book is about. That is what will make you far more skilled than most hypnotists in practice today.

In the House of Ideas... Conversation, Influence, and Persuasion

The first key to hypnosis is recognizing and utilizing these naturally occurring trance states in yourself and others.

The second key is knowing how to induce, or create, a trance in others **at your will**; and you can do it. I will teach you.

The best way to learn hypnosis is <u>using it in real life</u>.

Find yourself beginning to recognize the every day moments when people "zone out".

This is the first step.

<u>What are your beliefs?</u>

Most people who are overtly hypnotized for the first time tell me that it feels different than what they imagined. I agree.

The first time that I was hypnotized on purpose, I imagined that I would not remember a thing... like I had fallen asleep. I learned quickly that I had the wrong idea.

There is a misconception among the general public as to what hypnosis actually is.

This misconception comes from television, movies, and just plain ignorance.

Most people hold the belief that you are under the control of the hypnotist, and you are not aware of what is going on around you or what is being said.

While this is definitely possible, the feeling of control is misunderstood.

Control does not mean walking up to someone and saying, "You will buy me a High Definition Flat Screen TV... now," and they go and bring you back a new television.

It is not a fight of will powers or of mental strength between you and your subject.

The control comes from your ability to purposely direct the thoughts of your subject.

By directing your subject's thoughts, you direct their decisions, behaviors, and actions.

Personal Power is the ability that top leaders, celebrities, therapists, authority figures, and even con artists have developed.

Personal power is the ability to move people (even yourself) to take action.

Some people refer to this as charisma... the ability to arouse fervent popular devotion, enthusiasm, and action.

What sets personal power apart from charisma is focus.

Charisma is focused on how **others** perceive you.

> power is focused on how <u>others</u>
> you <u>as well as</u> how <u>you</u> perceive

This is very important, because the **key to hypnosis
is belief**... belief that you can do it, and your subject
WILL enter a trance and carry out your suggestions.

When beginning to learn hypnosis, many people have
a lack of belief about themselves and what is
possible.

They learn the techniques, but they do not get the
<u>results</u>.

It always comes down to belief.

**You will succeed <u>every time</u> as soon as you
develop the belief in yourself** that says, "<u>I know that
I can persuade this person</u>"; and you feel that belief
throughout every cell of your body <u>without any doubt</u>.

This **unstoppable confidence** is what separates a
bad hypnotist or entertainer or salesperson or
speaker or [fill in your profession] from a world-class
one.

When you make that shift in your internal belief
system, that is the point that you go from simply using
hypnosis to being a master communicator.

You must work on yourself before you can expect to influence others.

When I was introduced to hypnosis a long time ago, I did not have the belief system that I do now. As a matter of fact, I did not believe in hypnosis at all!

I watched my mentors and instructors make drastic changes in people. I even watched one of them call the play with 90% accuracy.

What do I mean by call the play?

Before walking into a business meeting with people we had never met, he would say, "I will get Barb to go out for donuts, Jim will scratch his nose within the first two minutes, and Tom will hand me $5.00."

Each of those things would happen exactly how he said they would happen.

Why and how could he get those results, and I could not?

Belief

It took me close to 50 times of being hypnotized before I developed the belief that hypnosis works, and I can do it. Now, I call the play; however, I am much more creative than having someone get me a donut or scratch their nose.

I want to speed your learning curve up.

I want you dedicated to working on yourself just as much as you are dedicated to being in front of a subject.

Work on your inner-game.

Make a list of things that you want or need to change or improve about yourself. Do you want or need to…

- gain more confidence,
- become assertive,
- be outgoing,
- overcome a fear or two,
- raise your motivation level,
- develop your personal power,
- lose some weight, or
- maybe something even more personal?

This book is designed to compensate for the fact that you are not in one of my boot camps.

Always complete the exercises and practice what you learn in the real world.

In my boot camps, the exercises are done during class, and we spend the evenings in the field using and perfecting the methods.

In the House of Ideas... Conversation, Influence, and Persuasion

The philosophy that we are using is <u>constant improvement over time</u>. Each of the skills and methods that you learn will build on one another. It is important to learn and master each small skill before the next lesson.

You will possibly be doing something that is different and uncomfortable to you. This means that you are <u>hitting the ceiling</u> that you have built for yourself. You can either bounce back down to your comfort level or push the ceiling higher.

If you fill a jar with flies, and cover the jar with plastic wrap; you can watch the flies repeatedly bounce off the plastic *ceiling* trying to get out.

Leave the jar with the flies in it for 24-hours. There is enough oxygen inside to sustain the flies.

24-hours later, you will see that the flies no longer bounce off of the *ceiling* that you have created for them. **They have developed a belief** (as simple as a fly's belief can be) that they cannot escape from the jar.

Now, take the plastic off.

Surprisingly, you will discover that the flies will not even attempt to fly out of the jar, because they have been conditioned by the plastic *ceiling*.

Be smarter than a fly.

Push your ceiling higher and higher. **It will move!** This is the only way that you can expand your skills and master anything.

Oh, the example I gave earlier... <u>"You will buy me a High Definition Flat Screen TV... now."</u> **The HDTV is on the wall in my bedroom.**

How will your life be when you can do that too?

Develop Rapport… The Right Way

In this lesson, you will learn one of the most important tools used to influence other people. Perhaps, <u>the</u> most important tool.

Remember the last time you were sitting with a friend doing whatever it is that you do with your friends, and they yawned. What happened?

Most likely, you yawned too.

You may have even said, "Stop yawning, because you're gonna make me yawn."

How can someone make you yawn? Why is that a common occurrence with virtually everyone on the planet?

It is as if you felt some kind of <u>connection</u> with this other person. Almost as if you were <u>in sync</u>.

And it does not even have to be a friend. It could be someone you just met on the subway, sat next to at a bar, or even saw on television.

Really think about that time, and ask yourself what it was that made you feel so in sync with that other person.

- Maybe you discovered that you had common interests with this other person.
- Perhaps you had a similar accent or other speech pattern.
- Did you come from the same hometown, the same school, or even the same neighborhood?
- Your beliefs about different things may have been the same.

It does not matter what it was; it comes down to the most important skill used to influence other people...

Rapport

I know what you are thinking... **"Not another lesson on rapport!"**

I understand! Rapport has been so overdone, but it has been **overdone** <u>incorrectly</u>.

If you skip over this lesson, because "you've heard it all"; you will miss out on what others have never taught you.

I find that most people have heard the term
some point. It is tossed around a lot in bu'
sales circles. Virtually every sales trainer I
speak touts the importance of building rappo,, ..

Here are two very simple yet very effective rules that I
use to create rapport:

1
When two people are like each other, they tend to like each other.

2
Imagine the person you are speaking with is the most fascinating person in the world.

Rapport is the ability to see the world as your subject
sees the world, to give him the realization that you
understand him, and to build such a strong bond with
him that he willingly wants to follow your suggestions.

Earn their trust, Create a bond, and Direct their thoughts!

Opposites Attract... BS!

How many times have you heard that "opposites attract"?

Opposites <u>do not</u> attract! They do add more excitement and uncertainty to each other's lives. Maybe that is the draw.

Think about it! Do you really want to spend time with someone with whom you have nothing in common? Is it fun to disagree about everything? What if they want to vacation in Alaska and you love Hawaii?

It does not seem like a good match, does it? Not at all!

You want to be with people who are like you!

You do not hang out at a comic book convention if you are not into comic books, do you?

So, how do you create rapport with someone?

There are a lot of ways to create rapport with someone, but it comes down to <u>creating things in common</u>. That is right... I said "<u>creating</u>".

Most people attempt to create rapport with others by <u>finding</u> things in common. You will hear things like...

- "What's your sign?"
- "Is that your trophy? I play softball also!"
- "Oh, really? I love Hawaii, too!"
- "So, what do you do?"

- "Where did you grow up?"

How many stock phrases can you come up with that you use on a regular basis?

Whoever said that you have to <u>find</u> things in common through the exchange of words and information?

What you really want is the emotional state of rapport... of feeling in sync with your subject.

Studies have shown that the <u>communication of emotional states</u> can be broken down into three components: <u>words</u>, <u>voice quality</u>, and <u>body language</u>.

- 7% of communication is done with words.
- 38% of communication is done with voice quality.
- 55% of communication is done with body language.

That means that most of what you are communicating is **NOT** coming out of your mouth. Surprised?

Didn't your parents just have a "look"? I mean, when you got this "look", you knew you had better do what they said. It wasn't about the words; it was about "the look". Perhaps, it was <u>the way</u> that they said it that alerted you that they meant business.

Let me give you another example... Two people can tell the same joke with exactly the same words yet get different reactions. Why?

It is more about your voice quality and your body language as you deliver the joke and less about the words.

Great comedians can take a story that is not funny and make it funny just by their delivery.

By only focusing on words and verbal information, you are ignoring the largest way to gain rapport with your subject.

It is much quicker and more effective to gain rapport with your subject through body language and your voice.

You can gain a very strong state of rapport by mirroring (copying) their breathing rate, their posture, their gestures, their tone of voice, the speed at which they speak, et cetera.

And you can create this connection within minutes and even seconds **without your subject's conscious awareness**.

Body language and voice qualities speak to your subject's unconscious mind... the part of the mind that you want to direct.

Words speak to your subject's conscious mind, and they actually keep the conscious mind busy while you direct their unconscious mind. When mirroring body language and voice qualities, your subject's unconscious mind begins to think, "This person is just like me. I like him."

As soon as that happens, a bond is created that grows stronger and stronger until you choose to break it... if you should ever want. (And there are times that you will.)

Your subject is not even aware of what is going on, because **you are relating to his unconscious**.

While your subject may know about rapport, he most likely only knows about creating it through words; and you are secretly building the bond without his conscious knowledge.

Here is a list of body language and voice qualities that you can mirror. This is not a comprehensive list, but it will give you a good start...

- Breathing
- Head Position
- Facial Movements
- Gestures
- Posture
- Eyebrow Movements
- Weight Shifts
- Foot Movement and Position
- Eye Contact
- Loudness of Speech
- Pitch of Voice
- Tone of Voice

• Rate of Speech

Remember, **anything you can physically mirror will work**.

In my boot camps, we conduct a mirroring experiment. Feel free to find a couple of friends, and experiment on your own.

This experiment requires three people. We will call them A, B, and C.

1. Person A thinks of a powerful memory. A memory that holds deep emotion. For the purposes of this experiment, find a positive memory.
2. Person A keeps this memory a secret, but he fully associates with this memory. In other words, he re-experiences this memory as if he was actually there by seeing what he saw, hearing what he heard, and feeling what he felt. (If there are any smells or tastes, experience those also.)
3. Person A stays in that memory and moves his body or sits or stands in the same posture as if he was actually experiencing the original event.
4. Person B mirrors everything that he can observe about Person A's body language. (Refer to the list above for ideas.)
5. Person C assists Person B by helping him assume the same posture and/or movements as Person A.
6. Do this for five minutes.

7. At the end of five minutes, ask Person B what emotion(s) he is feeling.
8. Ask Person A what emotion(s) he is feeling.
9. Ask Person B what he is thinking about.
10. Ask Person A what the memory was.

When doing this experiment in my boot camps, Person B can name the emotion(s) that Person A is experiencing with 95% accuracy.

Even more amazing, Person B can describe Person A's memory with 75% accuracy BEFORE Person A reveals what he was thinking about.

What would it be like if you could do this with any subject you choose? ... You can!

Develop your ability to observe, and be flexible enough to mirror your subject.

Now, you need to **find subjects and practice**.

I am giving you a mission...

1. Purposely create rapport with everyone possible.
2. Use body language and voice qualities instead of only words.
3. Your ultimate goal is to get someone (ideally, a complete stranger) to say something like, "It

feels like I have known you forever" or "I don't know what it is, but I just enjoy being around you" or "I feel so comfortable talking to you".

Learn to make your subject yell, "Suck It!"

I received the following email from one of my students...

Bill,

I had a situation at the office today.

A client misunderstood a clause in our contract, and he came into the office irate.

The first thing that I thought of was rapport since that's what I am learning right now.

The problem... How do you get rapport with someone in an angry and agitated state?

Please Help,
Dave
Tampa, FL

You have a few options with an angry and agitated person. Let's address your question with regards to

_ in rapport with an angry and agitated person, you mirror them just like you would anyone else.

The key is <u>not</u> to escalate their anger, but to express anger with them.

In other words, instead of expressing anger back at them, **direct your anger to the same topic that your subject is expressing anger towards**.

Terms to know…

PACING
The process of stepping into the behavior of another person.

LEADING
The process of another person stepping into your behavior.

In the situation described in the email above, you would express anger towards the fact that the clause in the contract was misunderstood.

Maybe you could have said (in an agitated state), "I hate when I misunderstand things like that. Just the other day I bought a DVD player just because it had a rebate. When I got it home and went to fill out the rebate, I realized that I had to also buy one of the DVDs that they had listed on the back of the form. I was so angry at myself for not reading that beforehand!"

Now, you are mirroring his state <u>AND</u> you have developed a common experience. That is a good foundation to deepen the rapport. Remember, the goal is to lead.

After establishing enough rapport, change your state; and lead your subject to a state of calm and understanding.

You may be thinking to yourself, "But I never bought a DVD player the other day!"

This is called **utilization**, and I will talk about that in a moment.

If you are having an ethical or moral dilemma about "lying" to your subject, then look at it this way...

You are not lying, you are simply utilizing your skills by using metaphor to develop rapport and take control of the situation and your subject.

What if the subject is expressing anger towards you?

Same thing... express anger towards the same topic as your subject. In this case, that topic just happens to be you.

If the subject is expressing anger towards you, then say something in an agitated state like, "I know! I cannot believe that my explanation did not clarify the clause well enough! That is why I make it a point to read through each contract I sign and ask questions if I do not understand something. I learned my lesson just the other day. I bought a DVD player just because it had a rebate. When I got it home and went to fill out the rebate, I realized that I had to also purchase one of the DVDs that they had listed on the back of the form. I was so angry at myself for not reading that beforehand!"

In this example, you have successfully directed your anger towards the topic of your subject... you, and you have turned it into a rapport building experience.
Just stay calm, and watch closely. Do not escalate your subject's anger towards you unless you know how to take and stay in control of the situation.

Keep practicing, and you will master all of the skills needed to defuse this type of situation.

I mentioned the term **utilization**.

About two nights ago, the telephone rings; and I answer. I say, "Right on time!"

My sister asks, "What?"

NOTE: At this point, I know it is my sister; because she said the word "what", and I recognized her voice. Also, the caller's phone number pops up on the phone.

So, I repeat, "Right on time!"

She asks, "For what?"

I explain, "Well, I needed to ask you a question, so I sat down and concentrated on both the question and you. Within 60 seconds, the phone rang. May I ask what you called for?"

She said, "I called to tell you what time we'd be at your home tomorrow."

I exclaimed, "Exactly! That's what I needed to know!"

There was a 15-second period of silence in which my sister is processing how I could have made her call me.

This is very enjoyable for me!

What she has not realized is that I did not "predict" a thing.

It was simply a matter of <u>pacing</u> her, <u>leading</u> her, and <u>utilizing</u> what she told me to give the impression that I made her call to answer my question.

By doing this, I have also reinforced the belief in her that I have some kind of "power" that is not natural. She remains very leery of me. Just as a good brother-sister relationship should be.

If this were a complete stranger on the other end of the phone, this process would have begun to build the belief that I have supernatural powers.

This is my belief that **I** want to install... **my** personality.

What beliefs do you want to install in your subjects quickly?

Utilization is the key to not only building a connection and deepening the rapport with your subject; it is also a magic formula to quickly put your subject into a trance, install beliefs in your subject, and influence your subject. It is not **the** magic formula, but it is one magic formula.

As I demonstrated in my response to Dave's email

above, I utilized what my subject was telling me (both verbally and non-verbally) to move him in the direction that I wanted him to go.

Let me give you another example.

For some reason, I found myself sitting in a church one Sunday morning; and on this particular Sunday, the sermon seemed to really "move" some people.

In the row ahead of me was an old woman who suddenly raised her hands to the sky and yelled, "Amen!"

She then closed her eyes and left her hands high in the air.

Another, "Amen!", and then a "Hallelujah!"

I can recognize a trance when I see one; and when I recognize one, I am like a kid in a toy store. I have to play with it!

I slid down the pew until I was right behind her.

I leaned up, and I whispered in her ear, "As your hands reach toward the heavens, you can now feel the power flowing through your body."

NOTE: I am utilizing what she is already doing... raising her hands in the air!

She yells again, "Amen!"

I continue, "That feeling inside grows and flows

through you until it just wants to burst out."

Another, "Amen!"

I continue, "You need to let it out, but not yet. You need to let it out in a very specific way. Can I get an 'Amen!'?"

She complies with another, "Amen!"

NOTE: At this point, I have rapport, because she is complying with my suggestion to give me another "Amen!"; and I am utilizing her current experience to direct her to perform my little Sunday morning persuasion experiment.

I then say, "He wants you to show everyone in this room that you feel his presence and his spirit in and around you by jumping up and yelling the words that you hear whispered in your right ear in a moment, and you'll do this without any conscious thought on your part! Give me an 'Amen!'"

My subject's head begins shaking "yes", she gives me the "Amen!", and her muscles tense up ready to spring from her seat.

I lean over to her right ear, and I say, "Suck It!"

She jumps to her feet, and yells louder than any "Amen!" before, "Suck It!".

Everyone in the church turns and looks at h

I am holding in laughter, she is feeling the
everyone else is instantly in a trance called "dısฺฺ.

This is utilization!

Utilization is not an exact science... it is more of an art.

Essentially...

Pay attention to your subject instead of the crap inside <u>your</u> <u>own</u> head!

If you do this, you will gain more information from your subject than you ever imagined.

Use this information for your advantage.

Learn to instantly direct your subject's thoughts and emotional states!

Imagine driving down the road, and you suddenly see the flashing lights of a state trooper in your rear view mirror. What happens?

- You get a rush of adrenaline,
- Your heart begins to race,
- Your breathing changes,
- You get a sinking sensation throughout your body, and
- Thoughts about what is about to go down flood your mind.

Then, the state trooper passes you and speeds ahead. All of this happened, because you simply saw the lights. You may even have experienced some of these things just reading this. Why?

An anchor was unconsciously fired off.

So, what is an anchor?

An anchor is formed when an internal response becomes associated with an external stimulus. Think Pavlov and his salivating dogs...

Hear A Bell = Salivate

In the above example, the external stimulus is the flashing lights behind you; and your internal responses are the adrenaline, heart, breathing, and emotional changes that you feel.

A phobia is an example of a powerful anchor. In most cases, a phobia is established in a single, brief, and intense learning experience. From that point on, when the external stimulus happens, the phobic response kicks in.

Here is the kicker...

The stimulus can be virtually unnoticeable or even out of conscious awareness, and the response can be either positive or negative.

How does this apply to you?

Imagine your subject is the CEO of a company, and you have an appointment with him and a few of his employees to present your ideas.

You arrive at his office, and his assistant walks you back to the conference room so you can set up.

Walking into the conference room, you see a long conference table.

You "innocently" ask the CEO's assistant, "Where does the decision maker sit?"

She points to the chair that the CEO normally sits in and says, "He sits right there." She walks out of the room.

What do you do?

You set up your presentation at the chair that the decision maker (in this case, the CEO) sits in, and you sit in his chair.

That particular position at the table is already **anchored** to <u>power</u>. When the CEO makes a decision or suggestion, it is listened to and most likely carried out without question whether others agree or not.

By sitting in the CEO's chair, you unconsciously <u>link</u> those feelings of power that the employees normally associate with the CEO to yourself.

All of the power that the CEO commands from his employees is now transferred to you.

When you present, they will listen and likely agree with you... even the CEO.

In a very short period of time, the CEO's power becomes anchored to you, and you will command the same respect if you are near the CEO's "spot" at the table or not.

In other words, not only does the CEO's chair cause the employees to access those feelings, but <u>you</u> also cause the employees to access those feelings... <u>if you anchor them correctly</u>.

That's the power of anchors!

Won't the CEO have a problem with you sitting in his chair?

Not at all, if you have remembered to build rapport from the beginning.

By having a strong connection and creating rapport with your subject, you earn his trust and respect. He will let you sit in his chair.

If he kicks your butt out of his chair, then you have not developed a strong rapport. Go back, and get that connection.

It helps if rapport is present through everything that you do.

The steps to anchoring your subject...

1
Determine what internal response (state) you want your subject to experience on your command.

In the example above, maybe the states of slight intimidation, a feeling of respect towards you, and possibly even a "yes man" state in your subjects would be useful.

Your goal state(s) that you want your subject to experience will be different depending on your situation and your desired outcome.

For example, suppose you want your significant other to feel absolutely <u>turned on</u> with a slight touch of your hand or with a certain word that you say in a seductive way. This is very different from the example above (and a lot more fun), but the steps to create the anchor are the same.

2
Get your subject to experience the specific state that you have chosen.

There are a couple of ways to do this:

1. Utilize an existing anchor as we've done in the example above. The existing anchor in

> this example is the associations that the employee's have with the CEO's position at the table.
>
> 2. Create the states in your subject by crafting your language.

Let's first concentrate on utilizing existing anchors.

In the boardroom example, the CEO's position at the table is the existing anchor. By simply sitting in his chair, you fire off the anchors that his employee's have associated with his presence in that particular spot.

With your significant other, you can simply wait until they are at the peak of the goal state... the state of being absolutely turned on.

The more intense the state, the stronger the response will be when you "fire off" the anchor later.

3
Create the anchor.

The anchor can be some unique touch, sound, sight, smell, or taste. You can use one modality (sense) to anchor; and by using two or more of the modalities, you make the anchor even stronger.

The more <u>unique</u> the anchor, the more powerful it will be when fired off later; however, make it easy to duplicate.

To fire off the internal response (the state) with speed and precision, you must accurately replicate the external stimulus (the anchor).

Remember the flashing lights in your rear view mirror? Those are accurately replicated each time they are flashing behind you.

Think of a song that takes you back to an old fling. Perhaps a particular smell sends you back to your grandmother's home. Maybe even a tone of voice makes you cringe still today.

The anchor could be a phrase in a certain tone of voice. It could be a unique hand gesture as you say a certain word. The anchor could even be a simple touch on your subject's shoulder.

In creating an anchor... Timing Is Critical.

Your subject's state will reach a peak level very quickly and then it will die down slowly.

Watch your subject, and use your instinct.
Whether you are <u>inducing</u> a state within your subject, utilizing a naturally occurring state, or taking advantage of an existing anchor; you must set the

anchor right before your subject reaches their pe state.

To see a visual of the optimum timing, go to... http:// goo.gl/DM501

4
Test it!

Fire off the anchor, and watch what happens.

There are no failures, only results. If you do not receive the result that you want when firing off the anchor, go back and do it again.

Stacking Anchors

An anchor, if done correctly, is set the first time; but it never hurts to condition the response.

Every time your subject is in the peak of the goal state, you should set (reinforce) the anchor. This will assure that the anchor will produce the result that you want when you fire it off in a critical moment.

Each time you reinforce the anchor, that anchor gets stronger and stronger.

You also intensify the internal state that your subject will go to when the anchor is fired off.

Consider this...

What would happen if you stacked different states?

Perhaps instead of repeatedly reinforcing the turned on state in your significant other, what if you stacked several states on the same anchor?

Let me put this another way...

What if you could fire off an anchor by simply touching your significant other on the back of the neck; and this anchor instantly sent a flood of emotions through your subject like turned on, passion, love, adventure, exhilaration, and curiosity?

This is called stacking anchors, because you stack one anchor on top of another on top of another.

Would that be a good thing to have control of?

Use your imagination, and go practice anchoring!

Capture your subject's imagination.

Have you ever seen someone that you instantly had wanton desire for?

In other words, you just had to meet them!

The first time I noticed my wife, she walked around a corner; and it was impossible to take my eyes off of her... she took my breath away.

A flood of emotions, thoughts, images, and feelings rushed through my entire body.

I was looking at this woman walking towards me, and I was thinking that I **had** to meet her.

She simply captivated me.

You have also done this!

You have seen someone, and you became entranced. **How clearly can you remember one of those times... now?**

Take a moment, and experience that.

In the House of Ideas... Conversation, Influence, and Persuasion

You introduce yourself.

After a conversation, it is clear that this person is as beautiful on the inside as they are on the outside.

You go on your first date.

This is the start of a whole different process in your mind. You see, there is a difference between wanton desire and love.

You can have both at the same time, but there is a difference.

After your first date, you go home; and you began to imagine.

You imagined this person in your life.

I know you have done this before... you have met someone, you spent some time with them, and you went home and you imagined doing all sorts of things with this person and having all of the amazing feelings that go along with those thoughts.

Over and over again, your mind continues to sort through everything that attracts you to this person.

The more time you spend with this person and the more you think about this person, the more you feel a strong connection drawing you to them.

You get butterflies when you are near each other, your heart races when you think about them, and you get that feeling in your chest that radiates out to the rest of your body making you feel almost euphoric.

Your friends get phone calls just so you can te
about this person.

Songs on the radio remind you of them.

You fall in love with them.

You can feel this as I describe it to you, can't you?

Although you may not have had this exact
experience, you have had the experience of falling in
love; and you went through a similar process. As I am
telling you this story, you search your memories for an
experience of your own in which to relate.

As you think about your memory
as you read my story, your mind
and body begin to experience
those feelings and emotions all
over again.

You may have noticed how your breathing changed or
how your heart began to pound inside your chest or
how the euphoric feeling of being in love began to
move through your body.

These things happened, because...

Whatever you can get your subject to imagine, they will also enter the emotional states as if they were experiencing the actual event; because your_mind does not know the difference between what you vividly imagine and what actually happens.

I described the experience of falling in love, and this caused **you** to feel the state of love in yourself.

Keep in mind that you are reading words on a page, and you are feeling the state that I am describing.

In reality, I would put myself into a "love state" as I describe the experience to you.

You would hear my tonality and vocal qualities, and you would see my body language.

This would enhance your experience of the state much more than simply reading words on a page.

I would also watch you and notice how deeply you are feeling the state that I am describing.

<u>As I described my experience, you searched inside for your own memory; and you experienced those states.</u>

Thinking back to your lesson on anchoring, Step 2 is to get your subject to experience the specific state that you have chosen.

You can do this by utilizing an existing anchor, or you can create the state inside your subject.

You have just learned one way to create a state inside your subject... **Put yourself into the state that you want your subject to experience, and then describe the experience in "normal conversation" as I did.**

You can also create a state inside your subject by getting them to vividly imagine a past memory in which they experienced the goal state.

<u>I used this method also in my example</u> by writing things like, "How clearly can you remember one of those times now?"

In a normal conversation, I could very easily use this method as follows...

Me: "Can you remember a time when you felt totally confident and unstoppable?"

Subject: "Yes."

Me: "Can you remember a specific time?"

Subject: "Yes."

Me: "Tell me about that."

As your subject describes the time that they felt totally confident and unstoppable, they will experience those feelings all over again.

As soon as you recognize that your subject is at the peak of the state, you proceed to Step 3 of the anchoring process.

By anchoring the states that you elicit in your subject, you have instant access to those states by simply firing off the anchors.

What sort of states would you like to be able to instantly access in your subject?

Another very important advantage of using these methods to elicit states in your subject is the absolute breakdown of resistance.

Whatever you can get your subject to imagine is perceived by them to be their own thoughts.

Your subject <u>will not</u> resist your suggestions if they feel as if your suggestions were actually their own ideas.

In the next lesson, you will learn how to systematically elicit your subject's strategy for specific states and covertly walk them through the same strategy to produce the state at your will.

You will also learn how to use your language with such precision that you will bypass any resistance that your subject may have.

For now, you have more than enough information to go out and elicit specific states in your subject and anchor those states.

Go practice!

Make it fun!!!

Use your imagination!

What states could you elicit in your subject that would create absolute pleasure in their life?

Create amazing states in others, and you get even more in return.

Let's bake a cake.

Just like you use a recipe for baking a cake, you unconsciously use recipes for everything you do. These recipes are called strategies.

You began making strategies, or recipes, the moment you were born by putting sequences of internal and external experiences together, and you made something happen.

For example, you felt hungry, you instinctively knew to cry, and you were fed. This recipe produced a desirable result, and you learned to use it to get food on demand. Of course, you now have a different recipe when you feel hungry because, as an adult, it would be awkward to cry until you were fed.

You have recipes for everything you do — such as buying a new refrigerator, deciding where you will sit in a movie theater, and what to give your significant other for their birthday. And like baking a cake, the order of the ingredients is just as important as the ingredients themselves.

Essentially, a recipe is some that happens in your mind ⌐ body that produces a specific result.

Let me give you an example... Suppose I want to know someone's recipe for buying a house.

It's not about the ideal neighborhood, the preferred school district, or how many bathrooms they need. Instead, it's about their strategy to make a large purchase.

- Do they make a picture in their mind?
- Do they have a particular word or phrase that they say to themselves?
- Do they hear someone else's voice in their mind saying, "Buy the house!"?
- Do they have a certain feeling or emotion?

In other words, I want to know what is going on inside their mind.

Their recipe for buying a house may be...

1. I say to myself, "I want to buy a new house."
2. In my mind, I picture how I want my new house to look.
3. I jump online to look at photos of houses that fit the Image in my mind.
4. I then say to myself, "Let's go buy a house."

5. I call my realtor to look at houses that I have seen online.
6. While going through the houses, I get a feeling that this is my home.
7. I tell my realtor, "This is the one."

At this point, many humans ask, **"That sounds great, but how do you find out someone's recipe?"**

Answer… **"You ask."**

Staying with the house example, I would ask, "What is the first thing you do when you decide to buy a new house?" And they would answer, "I want to buy a new house."

I would then ask, "After you say to yourself, 'I want to buy a new house,' what do you do next?"

This inquiry would continue until we reach the last step of the recipe — the step at which the buyer in the example above says, "I'll take it!." That is the end of the recipe — the buying strategy.

And then at this point, many people ask, **"Do people really tell you this?"**

Answer… **"Yes."**

If you have rapport and know how to hold a conversation, you will have very little resistance getting your subject to open up and share their recipe.

Stay relaxed, and start a conversation, "When you bought your last house, what was the first thing you did?"

If this is their first house, come up with something similar. For example, ask them about the last car they purchased, their previous refrigerator, or the diamond ring on their finger. There is an excellent chance that their buying recipe is similar regardless of the item being purchased.

There are only six ingredients that can go into a recipe. You can do each of these things internally or externally — and more than once.

1. Pictures
2. Sounds
3. Feelings
4. Tastes
5. Smells
6. You can talk to yourself

You will want to remember the order in which the ingredients happen. If you need clarification on a specific ingredient or order, slow your subject down and ask questions. You want to ensure that all the ingredients are in the recipe and the correct order.

After you learn someone's recipe, the most challenging part is over. Now, you simply have to take them through their recipe with the content that applies to the current situation.

For example, perhaps you learned your subject's recipe for buying a dishwasher; but you are selling a house. Simply take your subject through their recipe while substituting the house in place of the dishwasher.

Learning someone's recipe (strategy) and then taking them back through it while adding different content takes some practice — just like every other skill you've learned. Initially, it will be challenging to elicit and use your subject's recipe. However, the more you make yourself uncomfortable by asking the right questions and practicing new skills, the faster you will master conversation, influence, and persuasion.

I recommend asking friends to help you practice. Have them think of something they do (buying something, falling in love, picking a movie, et cetera), and discover their recipe.

Go practice, feel uncomfortable, and master this skill. Before long, you will be eliciting and utilizing recipes without thinking about it.

When was the last time that you felt stuck?

I was in the bookstore last week. I often stop in just to see what new books are on the shelf on the subject of influence, sales, speaking, et cetera.

The section where these books are located just happens to be near the *self-help, put-your-marriage-back-together* section; and it never fails... there is always a couple standing in the aisle trying to agree on which book is best.

The inability to agree and compromise is what brings people to this section in the first place thinking that they can agree and compromise on the best book to buy to fix their problems. Instead, they find themselves acting out in a public place.

On this day, there was a particularly annoying couple who needed a lot more than a book to help their marriage. The bookstore is fairly large, yet people from the other end of the store were watching how the situation was unfolding. The conversation quickly went from, "You never respect my input," to "I bet you had the time to listen to your girlfriend when she said something!"

This situation was violating one of my rules of life...
Avoid Stupid People!

I had nowhere to go, however, because these two numbskulls were arguing in *my* aisle. I intervened.

I took two business cards out of my pocket, I walked up to the couple, and I said, "You can stand here and argue about what book will fix your problems or about who left the toilet seat up or who left the clothes on the bedroom floor or who slept with who, or you can begin to think about how good it feels to be in love with each other... now."

An instant trance was developed in both of them as they stood there and just stared at me for at least ten seconds.

What I achieved was an instant induction. It creates a great opportunity to give direct suggestions to your subject.

I reached out to each of them, grabbed their hands, and I placed my business card between their fingers. I then looked at them and said, "Go home, get in bed, hold each other for a very long time, and call me to make an appointment in two days."

They stood there staring for a moment longer, they looked at each other, and then they left.

I received a call from them a couple of d
they scheduled an appointment. I am
did everything else I told them to do fir'

What I utilized is called a **transderivational se**
the process in which your subject must search
their memories for their own meaning of what you
are explaining to them or what they are
experiencing.

In the example above, the couple had just been told
by me, <u>a stranger</u>, to think about how good it feels to
hold each other.

As they stood there staring, they were attempting to
put meaning to the fact that a stranger walked up to
them and told them to get in bed with each other.

Transderivational search can be utilized to create
a deep trance, because it is an automatic and
unconscious state of internal focus.

The best part...

Your subject will never see it
coming.

Everything a person hears, sees, feels, or
experiences in any way produces a
transderivational search.

This produces a trance.

To take this a step further, this means that every word that a person hears produces at least a brief transderivational search.

That means that you have been putting people into trances since the first instant you could communicate.

The moment your subject begins to process and interpret what you are saying or doing by searching their memories for meaning, you have induced a trance.

You have learned how to capture your subject's imagination by activating a memory search in a previous lesson.

In this lesson, you will learn how to create instant trance and directly affect your subject's thoughts using this same method.

You may have heard of the **handshake induction**. If you have not, it is simply a hypnotic induction in which a trance is produced during a handshake.

It is quick, it is effective, and it takes guts to carry out.

Confusion is the basis for this trance induction... much like the confusion that I created in the couple when I told them to get in bed.

Many actions that you carry out on a daily basis are learned as a single "chunk" of behavior.

Shaking hands is a great example of this.

There is no beginning, middle, or end to a handshake. **A handshake is one fluid, unconscious movement.**

Think about it! If someone walks up to you and extends their arm to shake hands, then your hand automatically reaches for theirs to complete the handshake. It is all unconscious movement!

In high school, we used to play this game where we would reach out to shake hands with someone; and then at the last moment, we would pull our hands back and say, "Psych!". Do you remember doing this?

The other person would stand there with an outstretched arm for a brief moment not knowing what to do.

An automatic behavior had successfully been interrupted. This forced the subject to enter a transderivational search to determine what this means and what to do next.

The mind deals with this interruption by putting itself into a trance until either something happens to give a new direction or until it figures out what to do on its own.

Some people would stand there for a second, and others would stand there for five, seven, ten, or more.

The amount of time that the subject stood there with their arm outstretched was the time it took for them to perform a transderivational search, put meaning to what just happened, and determine what to do next.
What I did not know in high school is that this is precisely the amount of time that the subject is highly suggestible, and this moment can be utilized to produce a deeper trance.

The Handshake Induction...

1. Make sure you are in a very confident state. The Handshake Induction is not for the faint of heart.
2. Reach out to shake your subject's hand with your right hand (as you normally would).
3. As your subject reaches for your right hand and just before your two hands connect, pull your right hand slightly back.
4. In one fluid movement, lightly grasp your subject's right wrist with your left hand; and move your subject's right hand up in front of their face while pointing to their hand with your right index finger.
5. Immediately give suggestions to "look at your hand and notice the changing focus of your eyes as you allow those eyelids to close and simply listen to the sound of my voice".
6. If done with confidence and without hesitation, you will produce a deep trance.

What you do with this trance is up to you.

Take some time to watch this instructional video on how to conduct the handshake induction… https://youtu.be/QHujLb9MH_0

This works, because…

You have forced your subject into a transderivational search to find a meaning to what the hell is going on.

You stopped an action that should have been automatic, and you have given a new direction by raising their hand to their face and telling them to close their eyes.

Their mind has no program for this, and your subject is essentially letting you write the program for them.

Do you have the guts to give this a try with complete and utter confidence?

If you are not able to build up your confidence, apply what you already know... **anchoring**. You have learned in past lessons how to anchor your subject. Apply this same technology to yourself.

In the next lesson, I will explain in detail how to place anchors on yourself to instantly access any state that you want… at will.

A handshake is not the only way to produce a deep trance using the phenomenon of transderivational search.

Anything that forces your subject to go inside and find meaning to what is being said or what is happening will work.

Think confusion!

Confusion is ultimately what we are producing here, and confusion very quickly leads to trance.

My telling the couple to get in bed with each other produced confusion to which they had to give meaning. While they were in a trance induced by a transderivational search, I gave them suggestions that they very accurately carried out.

They had to find meaning and a direction to move from the confusion that I had created.

To give you another example… I was sitting on a plane waiting for takeoff. Next to me was a woman who was clearly afraid of flying.

I played the situation out in my head, and I had two choices:

1. I could be miserable for ho'
   woman freaking out next to me,
2. I could drop this woman intc
   deal with her fear before we tc

I looked at her and said, "It seems that you hav~ some issue with flying."

She said, "Yes, I'm terrified."

I replied with, "How can you be so terrified of flying when you really have to concentrate on the space at the center of the small of your back when you're in the air?"

Immediately, this woman started a transderivational search to make some kind of sense out of what I had just asked her, and she dropped into a deep trance.

While she was staring straight at me, I said, "Close your eyes for a moment, and get rid of that fear once and for all."

She closed her eyes, and I did a very brief coaching session with her.

Without overtly telling my subject that I am a hypnotist or that we were going to use hypnosis, I produced a deep and profound trance in her with one single question.

On another occasion, I was speaking with a woman who was complaining about the symptoms of menopause and how she just could not take it anymore.

Not wanting to sit and listen to this go on and on, I said, "I know what you mean. When I went through menopause, it was a bitch." Keep in mind that I was a thirty-something white guy at the time.

This confusion drove her deep into a transderivational search, she developed trance, and I said, "Now, just let those things that you were about to discuss find themselves being locked into the deepest part of your mind where there is no need to speak about them with me ever again."

She looked at me and said, "I'm sorry. I spaced out for a second there. What were we talking about?"

Begin to notice the automatic behaviors that are common to every day life... like a handshake, tying your shoes, opening a door, smoking a cigarette, et cetera...

When you notice these automatic behaviors, **you can begin to interrupt them**, and begin to artfully structure your communication to create confusion in your subject.

These skills will allow you to masterfully send your subject into a transderivational search and produce deep trance.

<u>Anchor yourself to total confidence!</u>

Did you have the guts to elicit some deep **transderivational searches**?

If you found yourself needing a little more confidence and assertiveness, then this is the lesson for you.

You already know how to anchor other people, so let's anchor **YOU**!

Anchoring yourself is very easy to do. As a matter of fact, you have done it many times in your life.

You have even anchored yourself without your conscious awareness.

Is there an adult beverage that you just cannot drink?

I have one!... Apple Pucker. I drank two 2-liters one night... by myself. Now, simply smelling the stuff will send me running for the bathroom.

Apple Pucker is an anchor for me.

Perhaps you have fears... those are anchors. You are born with only two fears... the fear of falling and the fear of loud noises.

Every other fear that you have you learned somewhere along the way.

These are anchors.

For example, many people have the irrational fear of spiders. They see a spider, and they automatically exhibit the fear.

The spider is the anchor, and it puts into motion a set of emotional and physical reactions without any conscious involvement.

What are some anchors that you have?

If you can set an anchor on yourself on accident, then you can surely set an anchor on yourself on purpose.

Setting positive anchors on yourself is the most powerful and immediate way to improve your love life… your business… you name it.

Suppose you just completed something of which you are totally proud. How do you feel at that moment?

You feel at the peak of your game… confident… in *the zone*.

Anchor that state!

Follow the steps that you would use to anchor a subject, and anchor yourself instead.

When you are feeling at the top of your game, do something unique. Maybe you could make a fist and say "YES!" in a very passionate voice.

By setting this anchor, you can instantly put yourself into a peak state… a confident state… in *the zone…* by simply firing off the anchor... make your fist and passionately say "YES!".

How valuable will this be?

Answer: VERY!

How would you like to set an anchor that will instantly create unstoppable confidence?

Your brain does not know the difference between what you vividly imagine and what actually happens.

A study was conducted using three groups of basketball players.

This study's goal was to improve their free throw shooting skills.

- **Group One** practiced free throw shots for thirty minutes every day for a week.
- **Group Two** could not practice, play, or even watch basketball on television for a week.
- **Group Three** simply closed their eyes and imagined that they were shooting free throws for thirty minutes a day.

At the end of the week, the players were tested.

Group Two's skills had deteriorated as you would expect, because they did not practice.

Group Three, who practiced only in their imaginations, improved significantly more than Group One who had practiced with a real ball every day.

Granted, each of these groups already had the physical ability and know-how when it came to shooting free throws.

The thing to write home to Mom about is the fact that you can improve your game by using your imagination.

And it gets even better!

The old adage that practice makes perfect is only partially true. In reality...

Perfect practice makes perfect!

And you can practice perfectly in your imagination.

By practicing perfectly in your mind and feeling that incredible rush, you have unlimited peak experiences at your disposal to use for your peak performance anchor!

Simply take some time with your imagination to ramp up your emotional state by visualizing yourself on top of your game. When you feel as if you are at the very peak of that state... you are in *the zone*, set the anchor on yourself.

Get creative!

You do not have to make a fist and yell "YES!"... unless that is what you really want to do.

What would happen if you ramped yourself into a peak state and then reached over and touched your right elbow?

And then what would happen if you did that five or ten times in a row?

What would happen is that you would create a very powerful peak performance anchor that would be fired off and instantly put you in *the zone* each time you touched your elbow.

How handy would that be, Skippy?

And do not stop there... **What other states would be valuable to immediately access at will?**

Would it be to your advantage to instantly have access to a feeling of calmness, clarity, extreme focus, or the ability to block everything and everyone out?

Anchors can be created for every state that you need to access.

- Touching your left wrist could be calmness,
- cracking your knuckles could bring on extreme focus,

- scratching your head could instantly give you clarity, and
- looking directly into your subject's eyes could allow you to spontaneously block everything and everyone else out.

Your imagination is the limit. <u>Let the possibilities be limitless!</u>

Do yourself a favor that will pay off big... set some anchors!

<u>Read this lesson, because you will learn something.</u>

The right word spoken in the right way at the right time can change the world.

The most critical skill you can master is your ability to <u>communicate with precision</u>.

Instead of using words to simply get your point across, **use words on purpose**.

Because of how the human mind works, you can very accurately predict the output by what you input.

Every single word initiates a **transderivational search**. When you can masterfully communicate to fire off a planned chain of transderivational searches inside of your subject, <u>you can make people think and do exactly what you desire</u>.

This is not as difficult as it may sound.

With over 28 years of focused study and experimentation on how people communicate and process that communication, **I have discovered predictable patterns that occur in everyone**.

The next several lessons will teach you these language patterns. Some of the patterns are very simple to learn and seem like commonsense, and others take some study and practice.

The practice will pay off! Just do it, learn it, and you will create amazing things in your life.

Language patterns are most effective when used in combination. You will learn them one at a time, and then you will learn to use them together.

Master one pattern, and move on to the next.

You will find that you automatically incorporate all of the language patterns you have mastered as you learn each new pattern.

Incantations are the magical spells that you see in SciFi movies, right? Sort of.

The dictionary definition of incantation is the uttering of words purporting to have magical powers.

I am telling you that **magic words do exist**. Repeating abracadabra, alakazam, hocus pocus, presto, or even shazam will not get you what you need, however.

The magic words that I am talking about are those words in the English language that have impact on the human mind.

Let's begin with one of those magic words right now.

Because I said so...

When you use the word "because", you greatly raise your chances of getting what you want.

It works, because people want to know why.

Dr. Ellen Langer, a professor in the Psychology Department at Harvard University, has focused much of her work on control and decision-making; and she conducted the following study.

Langer had the librarian at Harvard University shut down all but one copying machine in one of the busiest wings of the library. Very quickly, a long line had formed.

During the next several days, **Langer had other students approach subjects at the front of the line asking to "cut".** These requests were specifically worded in three different ways:

1. "Excuse me, may I use the Xerox machine; because I'm late to class?"

2. "Excuse me, may I use the Xerox machine?"
3. "Excuse me, may I use the Xerox machine; because I have to make some copies?"

"Excuse me, may I use the Xerox machine; because I'm late to class?"

By using this phrase, the subject allowed the student to "cut" in line **94%** of the time. Makes sense, right? The student had a legitimate reason, and it sounded nice.

"Excuse me, may I use the Xerox machine?"

Using this phrase ticked many subjects off. The subject had been standing in line for some time, so why would they let someone "cut" for no reason what-so-ever? With this phrase, the subject allowed the student to "cut" in line only **60%** of the time.

"Excuse me, may I use the Xerox machine; because I have to make some copies?"

Again, this phrase brings back a reason, but it does not appear to be a legitimate reason for the subject to allow the student to "cut" in line; however, the subject allowed the student to "cut" in line **93%** of the time. **That is only 1% less than the legitimate sounding reason above!**

It does not make sense, does it? Everyone in line had to make copies. What made this person any different?

It was the use of the word "because".

People operate in their own little trance most of the time. They take as many shortcuts as possible so they do not have to think any more than necessary.

When you hear the word "because", your mind automatically begins to process the statement or question. **Your mind assumes that the request is legitimate, simply because the word "because" is heard.** The word "because" is an anchor.

Using "because" in real life...

"Why don't I get your phone number, because I can call you?"

This sounds harmless, but what you are doing is stopping your subject from automatically coming up with an excuse to not give you their phone number.

"Bob, you'll find that I have answered any question that you may have, because I have gone over them with you."

Another harmless sounding statement, and all that Bob's mind will process is "you'll find that I have answered any question that you may have."

"Sarah, you always pay my way, because you pick up the tab."

Once again, effective, and it sounds harmless. Get the idea?

Go out, and try this for yourself; because you will find that it works wonders.

Most people you speak with will not even know that you are using this technique, because it is used so much in everyday communication on accident.

Master the "because factor", and you will notice an increase in your influence and charisma; because people will be carrying out your suggestions.

Did you notice that I used the "because factor" on you throughout this lesson?

DON'T TRY this at home.

The mind cannot not think of something. Does that make sense?

Let me put it another way.

If I tell you... "Don't think of a black cat." What happens?

You think of a black cat, don't you?

You may have thought of a black cat and scribbled out the image, immediately changed the black cat to some other animal, thought of something completely different after thinking of a black cat, or even imagined a black cat with a big, red slash through it.

However you **did not** think of a black cat, you **HAD** to think of one before you could not think of one.

Without your subject being aware of it, you are able to implant an idea into their mind and direct their thoughts simply by using the word "don't".

One of the two ways to change emotional state is <u>focus</u>.

- If you focus on good things, you tend to feel good.
- If you focus on bad things, you tend to feel bad.
- If you focus on adventurous things, you tend to feel adventurous.

Get it?!?

Your subject will move to the state that you wish to elicit if you systematically direct their thoughts to that state.

Just don't get too curious about how well this will work when you use it for the first time.

Using the word "don't" allows you to direct your subject's thoughts. It allows you to control what they are imagining as they continue their conversation with you.

Some examples...

- "Don't think of buying this until you weigh your options for a moment." — This forces your subject to imagine buying.
- "It's okay. Don't let it bother you." — This successfully gives the hypnotic suggestion to "let it bother you". It is a good way to teach someone a lesson.

• "Don't think that they are only in it for themselves." — This leads your subject into thinking that "'they' are in it for themselves".

Get the idea?

"Try" this on your subject...

In one of the Star Wars movies, Yoda tells Luke, "Don't try. Do!" (I know, bad geek example; but it is relevant.)

You will never accomplish anything by trying.

Let's do an exercise...

Place a pencil on a table and "try" to pick it up. <u>You cannot!</u>

You can either do something or not do something.

<u>"Try" has the assumption built into it that you might fail.</u>

By convincing your subject to "try", you have effectively directed their thoughts to the possibility of failing.

Using "try"...

- "Try to resist the idea of you and me having a great time." — This suggests that they will not be able to resist the idea of having a great time with you.
- "Try to get a good night's sleep." — This suggests the possibility of not getting a good night's sleep.
- "Try to put it out of your mind." — This suggests that they will not be able to put it out of their mind.
- "Hey, Tom, I'd like you to try to bring your sales up next month." — This suggests the possibility that Tom will not bring his sales up.

Remember, whatever you consistently focus on, you tend to get more of.

Using the words "don't" and "try" secretly forces your subject to focus on what you want them to focus on.

<u>Your goal is to covertly and consistently direct the thoughts of your subject in the direction that you want them to go.</u>

Consistency is key!

Although, "don't" and "try" seem small in the scheme of things, they make a big impact when used consistently in a conversation along with the other language patterns that you have learned and are about to learn.

By consistently using and compounding everything that you learn in this course, you will lead your subject where you want them.

Imagine what it will be like when you...

Continuing with language patterns, you are about to learn three powerful methods for directing your subject's thoughts.

"Imagine" for a moment...

I wonder if you can imagine for a moment successfully using everything that you learn in this book.

With each new person that you use your skills on, you develop more and more influence.

You anchor your subjects without even thinking about it, and you fire those anchors off easily when you need them.

You imagine what it will be like when you have become a master communicator.

How good does that feel?

It is amazing at how you can change your state just by imagining certain things, isn't it?

Go out and do the same thing on your subject!

Remember, <u>you are consistently directing your subject's thoughts</u>.

I just directed yours to successfully mastering and using what you are learning, and you felt good.

Have your subjects "imagine" exactly what you want them to imagine.

Imagine this example...

"Summer, I wonder if **you can <u>imagine</u>** what it will be like when **you have found the person that you want to spend the rest of your life with**. That one person who you either just know that he is 'the one', or that person who **you begin to realize is your soul mate** the more time you spend with him. Can you imagine how that feels... now?"

In this example, Summer's thoughts are directed to finding her soul mate. With anchoring and embedded commands (you will learn these if you have not

already), this can be a very powerful and rapid
induce a state of wanton desire in your subject.

What would it be like...

Similar to "imagine", the phrase "what would it be like"
will direct your subject's thoughts in the direction you
suggest.

I think a simple example will suffice...

"Tom, what would it be like to **find yourself hiring
me**, improving in the areas that would make a
difference in your life, and reaching your goals that
you thought were once impossible?"

When you...

"When you" assumes that your subject will do the
thing or experience the state that you suggest.

It is not a question of doubt.

"When you" sends your subject's thoughts in the
direction of whatever comes after.

"Hey, Kelly, when you find yourself thinking about
calling me later, my number is on this card."

What does chocolate have to do with persuasion?

Every word is an anchor that initiates a transderivational search.

The way that you process information is through your five senses, also known as **representational systems**.

      V - Visual (Seeing)
      A - Auditory (Hearing)
      K - Kinesthetic (Feeling)
      O - Olfactory (Smelling)
      G - Gustatory (Taste)

Since smelling and taste are so closely related, we can combine those two representational systems.

Every experience, memory, even word can be broken down into a 4-tuple... a description that is made of (V, A, K, O).

- How does it look?
- How does it sound?
- How does it feel (both physically and emotionally)?
- How does it smell (and taste)?

Let's take an example...

If you read the word...

CHOCOLATE

...you immediately have a representation of what it looks like, sounds like, feels like, and how it smells and tastes.

You may even begin to get certain feelings throughout your body that you associate with chocolate, you think of a moment that you ate chocolate, and you imagine a time when you tasted your favorite chocolate.

I have just fired off an anchor in you by simply writing the word "chocolate" on this page.

Understand?

If I write the word "dog", you instantly have a representation of "dog" in your mind.

Your representation may be similar or vastly different to someone sitting right next to you.

You could have a Beagle in your mind, and another person could have a Great Dane in his mind... big difference!

This is very important for you to remember as you strategically use your language on purpose.

Even the word "the" is an anchor.

How do you know what the word "the" means, and how do you make sense out if it when you hear or see the word?

Think about it.

Automatically and unconsciously, you get a feeling that the word "the" is the right word to use; and you place meaning to it without any conscious thought.

The process is so rapid, that it is out of conscious awareness; but when you hear or see the word "the", an anchor is fired off that initiates a transderivational search.

Just like any anchor, **each word fires off unique emotions, images, and thoughts in your subject**.

Many are common and predictable.

As you learn more and more, you may find that some language patterns work quicker or are more effective with certain people than with others.

Your goal must be to master all of these language patterns so you can covertly weave them into your conversations without consciously thinking about it.

In this lesson, you are going to learn two more powerful language patterns.

As you practice these new language patterns as well as all the patterns you have already learned, begin to notice how different people react as you utter certain words.

A person can...

By talking about some unnamed person, your subject drops all resistance to your suggestions.

<u>You are not really talking about them.</u>

Some examples...

"Dave, isn't it funny how **a person can** find themselves opening up to something new, and just things happen."

"Amy, **a person can** feel an incredible sense of connection with someone they met in a very short period of time, can't they." (Notice that I used a period instead of a question mark. This is deliberate, because I want to say this line as a command... not a question.)

"**A person can**, Brooke, find that place deep inside where validation from your friends doesn't matter; and you just let yourself get swept away in the real moment."

If you were to...

"**If you were to**" not only **bypasses all resistance**, but it also **immediately directs your subject's imagination to what you are describing**.

Some examples...

"Ed, **if you were to** go ahead and hire me as your coach, what would be the first thing we will work on?"

"**If you were to**, Valerie, allow yourself to go out with me, when would now be a good time to grab a coffee and talk."

"**If you were to** realize that the price is not high when you consider the return on investment that you'll receive, isn't now a good time to get started?"

Remember, a person can weave many patterns into a single conversation. If you were to master this skill, how much influence will you have over others?

How easily will you master this lesson?

You have been learning some specific phrases that you can incorporate into your everyday language.

These language patterns, when used consistently in a conversation, will **greatly increase the influence and control that you have over others**.

Think of it as **the art of speaking directly to the unconscious mind**.

When you do this, you **eliminate the conscious interference and resistance** that you may have experienced in the past.

Even in writing these lessons, I have weaved in numerous language patterns to help you learn at a much deeper level.

Now, you are going to learn in a more broad sense.

By learning the big picture, you will be able to design your own language patterns that fit into your speaking style.

Presuppositions

Presuppositions are assumptions.

If you have ever purchased a car at a dealership, then you have heard presuppositions.

Salesperson: "What color do you want your car in?"

This question assumes that you are buying the car.

This just pisses people off, because it is considered... well... something a used car salesperson would say.

There are ways, however, to effectively use presuppositions.

Think of presuppositions in terms of what must be true in order for language to makes sense.

If I say, "My cat fell off the dining room table last night."

To make sense out of this statement, you have to assume that...

- I have a cat
- I have a dining room table
- My cat was on the table

Easy, huh?

Well, here is a question that was used by pollsters in a Presidential election...

"Does it bother you that Dan Quayle used his family's

influence to dodge the draft?"

Think about this question... It does not n
answer "yes" or "no".

**Regardless of what you answer, <u>you must
unconsciously accept the fact that Quayle did
indeed use his family's influence to dodge the
draft</u>.**

That is the power of presuppositions.

Time

Time can be used to presuppose an idea. "**Before** I
design a program to meet your needs, we have to talk
about your particular situation." **This statement
assumes that a program is going to be designed.**

"**While** you're unconsciously learning this material at
a much deeper level than you're even aware of; make
sure that you practice in the field, because you will
want to also consciously structure your language."
**This statement <u>installs the idea</u> that you are
unconsciously learning this material at a much
deeper level than you're even aware.**

There are many "time" words. Here are some
examples...

- Before
- After
- During
- As
- Since

- Prior
- When
- While

Numbers

Numbers and sequence can be used to presuppose.

- First, second, third, et cetera
- Another

"You have just learned **another** way to gain influence over others." **This statement installs the fact that you have already learned at least one other way to gain influence over others.**

"**First**, let's finish this drink; then we can get out of here." **This statement presupposes that "we can get out of here" as long as drinks are finished first. If there is no resistance to finishing the drink, then there will likely be no resistance to getting out of here.**

Or

The classic assumptive close... "Do you want it delivered today **or** tomorrow?"

Again, this sounds like a pushy salesperson, but let's soften it up and make it effective.

"Tom, I don't know if you'll master this material quickly **or** after consistent practice, but you will find it invaluable." **This statement presupposes that Tom will master the material.**

"Karen, are you ready to start now **or** would you first like to test drive our program for a week." **This statement presupposes that Karen will start. It is a matter of now or after a test drive for a week.**

Awareness

"Are you **aware** of how you have become more charismatic since you have started this course?" **This question is simply a question of your awareness. The fact that you have become more charismatic is accepted and slips into your unconscious mind without resistance.**

"Have you **noticed** how relaxed we are together even though we just met?" **Using the word "notice" allows the suggestion that you are relaxed with me even though we just met to covertly be installed.**

Other examples...

- Know
- Realize
- Found

Adverbs And Adjectives

Examples...

- Deeply
- Easily
- Curious About

"How **quickly** can you get ready to go out?" **This question presupposes that you are going out. It is simply a matter of how quickly you can get ready.**

"How **easily** do you make friends with new people?" **This question presupposes that you make friends with new people. It is a question of how easily.**

Change Of Time Adverbs And Adjectives

Examples...

- Begin
- End
- Start
- Stop
- Continue
- Proceed
- Already
- Yet
- Still
- Anymore

"You simply have not learned to master it **yet**." **The "yet" at the end presupposes that you <u>will</u> learn to master it.**

"Are you **still** not admitting that you screwed up?" **There is not a question that you screwed up. The question is whether or not you are still not admitting it.**

"I bet you'll **continue** to become more and more intrigued with me." **Being intrigued with me has** already taken place. Now I am urging you to become more intrigued with me.

Commentary Adverbs And Adjectives

Examples...

- Fortunately
- Luckily
- Innocently
- Happily

"**Fortunately**, you already use these language patterns in normal conversation." **This statement installs the idea that you already use the language patterns.**

"**Luckily**, you have someone who will tell you facts and not confuse you with a 'sales technique'." **This statement installs the thought that you will be given the facts and not tricked into buying.**

You use presuppositions all the time.

Now, use presuppositions on purpose.

Spend the next several days practicing these language patterns; and see if you can notice how much your influence, control, and charisma improve.

How do you hold two conversations at the same time?

This lesson is part one on **indirect elicitation**.

If I had to pick only one skill that I could use, indirect elicitation would be that skill.

It is the art of communicating with precision and purpose, and the results appear magical.

Indirect elicitation is the skill of getting a desired response from your subject without their conscious awareness.

Let me illustrate this by example...

You: "I wonder what time it is."

Subject: "It's 9:03."

In this example, a statement was made that produced a response without directly asking for the response.

"I wonder what time it is" is a simple statement that demands no answer.

Most people, however, will unconsciously process this statement as a question and answer you.

This is a very elementary example, but it illustrates the process well.

Let's jump right in and examine the different ways to accomplish indirect elicitation.

Embedded Commands

Embedded commands are directives that are contained within a larger sentence structure and are marked out in some way.

Embedded commands are **very effective in installing ideas and suggestions** into your subject's mind.

This is not a skill that you turn on and turn off.

Embedded commands should be used throughout your conversation, because a single embedded command will not be readily recognized by your subject's unconscious mind.

Multiple embedded commands, however, result in a covert conversation being held with your subject's unconscious mind that is virtually impossible to resist.

Here is an example. The embedded commands, the unconscious conversation, are in bold...

"**You, like me,** can probably **put all your attention on the person you're talking to**. I **find it so fascinating** how two people can just lose themselves in conversation, and **build a connection** in such a short amount of time. You don't even have to think about how much you **enjoy this person**, because **everything seems so natural**. That's what I really enjoy about meeting new people."

The embedded commands in the above example are...

- You like me
- Put all your attention on the person you're talking to
- Find it so fascinating
- Build a connection
- Enjoy this person
- Everything seems so natural

By installing these suggestions directly into your subject's unconscious mind, **your subject adopts these ideas and actions without question and without conscious awareness**.

Simply saying the words in the example above is not enough. **Your subject's unconscious mind must recognize that you are communicating directly to it.**

The unconscious mind is aware of things to which your conscious mind does not pay close attention.

Some examples of things that your conscious mind does not pay close attention to are...

- Hand gestures
- Voice tone
- Volume
- Tempo of speech
- Eye contact
- Nonchalant touches

What makes an embedded command an embedded command is the cue that lets your subject's unconscious mind know that you are speaking directly to it.

You deliver an embedded command to your subject's unconscious mind by marking out the command with some non-verbal cue.

For example, your voice tone can be lower when you deliver the embedded commands than during the rest of the conversation.

Maybe you can say the embedded commands in a slightly louder voice.

Making a specific hand gesture while you say the embedded commands is always a good choice.

For maximum effect, simultaneously use two or more non-verbal cues at the same time.

The key... Your subject's conscious mind should not be aware of the cues you are giving to their unconscious mind, so keep them as nonchalant and natural as possible.

Consistency is important, so begin your conversations with a goal in mind.

Let's say you would like to urge your subject to scratch his head...

"I have found that learning these language patterns is very **hand**y. The confidence that I have gained as I learn is **uplifting**, and I know that I have just only **scratch**ed the surface. I have already noticed that I'm a step a**head** of the people I hold conversations with. I **feel** that this is going to help me reach the goals that I have set for myself, and help me **head** in the right direction."

See how easy you can work the embedded commands into an innocent conversation?

It simply takes practice to perform the non-verbal cues as you deliver the embedded command.

In my boot camps, you will practice using embedded commands until they become natural to carry out. Contact me directly to learn more about my boot camps and other programs. Go to Bill@HypnosisForHumans.com now.

With focused and consistent practice, you will be using embedded commands without much conscious effort on your part. You will find that using embedded commands becomes a natural way of communicating.

Take several days to practice using embedded commands in the real world before going any further. Each skill builds on the one before, and it is very important to master a skill before moving on to the next.

Most importantly, have fun in the process!

<u>I wonder if you know what an embedded question is.</u>

You should have spent several days practicing **embedded commands**. If you did not, I highly urge you to do so. **Embedded commands take practice**, because you really have to focus on how you speak when you first start to use them.

Not only do you have to focus on how you speak, but you have to add in the component of marking out your unconscious messages. I promise you that <u>with consistent practice, it becomes easier and easier</u>.

As a matter of fact, **using embedded commands will become as easy as holding a conversation has always been for you**. The hand gestures, voice tonalities, pauses, and every other method that you are using to mark out your embedded commands will become part of your normal communication style.

Continue to practice embedded
commands and all of the skills

that you are learning on a consistent basis, make small improvements on your method, and you will soon master what you used to think was difficult.

I received an email from a student that illustrates the importance of consistent improvement and the "never fail" attitude...

> Bill,
>
> The techniques did not work at first, and my first thought was to try something else or stop; but I didn't, and I reminded myself that the techniques work... I just did it wrong. So, I tried again, and VOILA!
>
> BM
> Columbus

Now, let's introduce **embedded questions** into your language skills.

Embedded questions allow you to give a command within a question... <u>even though it is not a question!</u>

Confused?

Let's take some examples...

- "I'm wondering what the weather is going to be like this week."
- "I'm curious if you can get that done quickly."
- "I'm sitting here asking myself if you are really committed to learning and using this material until you master it."
- "I wonder what time it is."

Do you recognize yet what each of these examples has in common?

Each of these examples is structurally **not a question**, but each is usually responded to *as if* **it is a question**.

You can use an embedded question to command your subject to take action... "I'm curious if <u>you want to meet me for coffee tomorrow</u>."

To make it even more powerful, **combine the embedded question with other language patterns** that you have already learned... "I'm curious how much <u>you want to meet me for coffee tomorrow</u>."

It is not a question as to whether your subject wants to meet you or not... it is now a question of **how much** they want to meet you.

Using an embedded question is a great way to ask something without your subject feeling like they are being put on the spot.

In a sales situation, for example, you could say, "I'm wondering what else you may need to help you <u>move</u>

forward with this contract."

You did not ask what else they needed, because many people perceive that as a "sales technique". Stated as an embedded question, however, your subject will not become defensive and guarded; because you did not fire off the negative anchor attached to the question perceived as a sales technique.

But why didn't you fire off the anchor?

You did not fire off the anchor, because your subject did not "hear" a question...

- **Questions** are formed by the pitch of your voice going up at the end of a sentence,
- **Statements** are made by keeping the pitch of your voice flat at the end of a sentence, and
- **Commands** are created by lowering the pitch of your voice at the end of a sentence.

Try it out for yourself... say a question, a statement, and a command out loud; and notice how you end the sentence.

Because of this, **your subject will not perceive the question being asked, because it is disguised as a statement... or even better, a <u>command</u>**.

If you train yourself to lower the pitch of your voice at the end of each sentence in a conversation,

you will activate the command center in your subject.

Activating the command center will unconsciously **make your subject more likely to follow your directions**; because they are hearing seemingly innocuous sentences as commands.

Your subject has no reason to throw up their guard. When you do give your command, it slips through to their unconscious mind without any resistance.

As with embedded commands, **it is much more effective if you mark out the command or question for your subject's unconscious mind**.

You can mark out the command or question with any of the methods that you have been using while practicing embedded commands.

Can you take a moment and read this lesson?

I was sitting in a restaurant when I overheard a couple conversing with each other. At one point, one of them asked the other, "Do you have the time?"

The reply, "Yes, I do."

That was it, and it **was** a correct response to the question. I realize that it was a smart-ass way to answer, but it **was** the correct answer.

Usually a person will answer this question by responding with the time. This is called a **conversational postulate**.

Conversational postulates are yes/no questions that usually elicit a response instead of a literal answer.

This is a great way to embed a command within a question. Typically, your subject will act upon the command without much thought.

Here are some examples of conversational postulates...

- "Do you know what time it is?"
- "Can you reach that box on the top shelf?"
- "Can you sign right here?"
- "Can I have your phone number?"
- "Do you have a pen?"

Conversational postulates may simply sound like semantics, **because they are**. You are learning how to systematically structure your language to gain tremendous influence over others. Every new skill that you learn when combined with the other methods will increase your ability to lead your subject to the outcome that you desire.

Never brush a skill off, because it seems "too easy".

You will find that you will notice huge responses in your subject from the simplest of skills. This happens, because **you are learning to use your language on purpose at the precise time** instead of on accident.

Practice by noticing how you and others already use conversational postulates, then design some conversational postulates of your own that will elicit specific responses from your subject.

After designing your own, go have fun and practice.

Be ambiguous, and get results.

I had parent-teacher conferences for my daughter when she was 7-years-old. I walked into her classroom, and I noticed a poster hanging on the far wall. The title of the poster was **"HOMOPHONES"**.

I have been teaching homophones to adults, but I had forgotten the elementary school name for them. I call them **Phonological Ambiguities**... as do my students. **Phonological Ambiguities** are simply words that sound alike but have different meanings.

For example... I, eye; right, write, rite; weight, wait; their, there, they're; red, read; et cetera

The poster on my daughter's classroom wall listed about sixty good ones; so I snapped a photo.

Follow this link to view the poster. I would recommend that you download it or print it off, because it is an excellent reference to learn **phonological ambiguities**... http://goo.gl/Wlerp

Why are phonological ambiguities important?

They are important, because **they force your subject to initiate a <u>transderivational search</u> in order to determine which word is supposed to fit into the sentence that just came out of your mouth**.

In addition to initiating the transderivational search, **phonological ambiguities** create confusion.

Confusion is one of the quickest ways to put your subject into a trance.

Also, <u>phonological ambiguities are a helluva lot of fun to use</u>.

I sat down with my daughter **and** her teacher. As of the writing of this book, the schools began within the last two years to turn parent-teacher conferences into <u>student-lead meetings</u> instead of just speaking with the parents alone. **My goal is to put the teachers into a trance and make them learn a few things themselves.**

About five years ago, I had a school that my children were attending pull the food pyramid from the classrooms.

Do you remember the food pyramid from your school days?

Do you know where it came from?

Do you still follow it?

The food pyramid was designed as a marketing tool by farmers to sell grain... grain makes up the largest portion of the pyramid... hence, farmers sell more product.

Did you know that <u>in 2005 the federal government ordered schools to take the pyramid out of the classroom</u>? It is not used anymore except on some food packaging for marketing purposes... its original intent anyway.

I look at my daughter's teacher, and I point to the homophones poster and say, "In the adult world, we call those phonological ambiguities."

She asked, "What?"

I replied, "Those... on the poster... those are phonological ambiguities."

She said, "No, those are homophones. We don't want to mess up the kids by teaching them something different."

So, I told her the story of the food pyramid and how I managed to get it taken out of a school.

She does not know that I am a hypnotist, so **she is not aware that I am leading her down my path**.

After my story, she said, "We may have a problem here."

I said as I pointed to myself, "Yes, we do... It's a parent." (NOTE: This is meant to be a phonological ambiguity.)

What she heard with her **conscious mind** was "Yes, we do... it's apparent."

What her **unconscious mind** understood was, "Yes, we do... it's a parent."

After a brief 10-minute meeting laced with hypnotic language, my daughter's teacher now has a slight **fear** of the term homophones; and she feels a whole lot of pleasure whenever she hears the term **phonological ambiguities**.

How can you work phonological ambiguities into everyday conversation to initiate a trance state?

First, have fun.

Second, list all of the ambiguities that you can think of, and work them into your normal conversations.

The link to the poster I mentioned earlier in this lesson will give you a great start.

Here are some examples. The "correct" word is in parentheses...

- "I have a home that I think you'll really like. Let's take my car and go buy (by) the house now."

- "As you read this lesson, you'll find that <u>you're (your)</u> unconscious begins to learn new things without your conscious awareness."
- "Just sit back for a spell (spell could mean a magical spell or a period of time), and let me tell you a story."

How ambiguous can you be?

In normal communication, it is often important to be specific. To be ambiguous causes confusion and misunderstanding.

When developing a trance in your subject, however, ambiguity is a very important tool.

Ambiguity creates confusion, confusion forces your subject to go inside their mind to find meaning to what you have just said, this going inside to find meaning is called a transderivational search, and you have successfully created a trance in your subject using ambiguity.

Syntactic Ambiguities occur when a sentence can be interpreted in more than one way or mean more than one thing. **Syntactic ambiguities** are not single words. They are created from the relationship between the words and the clauses of a sentence.

When your subject can interpret the same sentence as having

more than one meaning, then your statement is a syntactic ambiguity.

Simply keep in mind that using **syntactic ambiguities** creates a transderivational search in your subject that can be utilized.

Added to your arsenal of skills, syntactic ambiguities add a powerful impact.

Here are some examples to give you a better idea as to what syntactic ambiguities are, how they are created, and ways that you can use them in conversation with your subject...

- Flying planes can be dangerous. (Are flying planes dangerous, or is the act of flying planes dangerous?)
- Barb and Tom are visiting relatives. (Are Barb and Tom visiting some of their relatives, or are Barb and Tom relatives who visit?)
- The dog was found by a bench by a lady. (Did a lady find the dog by a bench, or was the dog found by a bench that was by a lady?)
- The woman tried to take a photo of a man with a flashlight. (Did the woman try to take a photo of a man who was holding a flashlight, or did the woman try to take a photo with a flashlight?)
- And let's finish off the examples with a quote by Groucho Marx... "Time flies like an arrow; fruit flies like a banana."

Syntactic ambiguities produce a trance state that you can utilize to move your subject in the direction that you want.

Have fun, write some out, use them, and notice the quick yet profound results that you get.

<u>Someone saw me with a telescope.</u>

Carrying on with our discussion on ambiguity... **Scope Ambiguity** is a handy tool to have in your box.

Keep in mind that ambiguity creates confusion, confusion forces your subject to go inside their mind to find meaning to what you have just said, this going inside to find meaning is called a transderivational search, and you have successfully created a trance in your subject using ambiguity.

Scope ambiguity happens when it is unclear how much a verb, adverb, or adjective applies to a sentence.

For example...

"Old men and women steal!"

Who steals in this example... Old men and old women OR old men and women?

It is difficult to determine... impossible to determine... to whom the "old" applies.

This may seem trivial, but what would happen if you added **scope ambiguity** into a conversation with all of the other skills that you are mastering?

You would be a flippin' master persuader… that is what would happen.

Suppose you were influencing a friend to be your "wingman" for the night, and you wanted to throw a **scope ambiguity** in the mix.

You could say...

"Dave, I promise you that there will be a beautiful woman for each of us."

This sentence creates at least a mild state of confusion, because...

Are there two beautiful women... one for each of us, or is there one beautiful woman who will be with each of us?

Depending on the true meaning of this sentence, Dave could have a surprise in store for him later that night!

Let's take one more example...

"That was a great group of fascinating women and men."

Who was fascinating... just the women or the women **and** the men?

Admittedly, this is not my favorite language pattern, but it is a tool that I pull out now and then.

<u>These produce very powerful results can come in simple methods.</u>

When my son was 6-years-old, he was already a master at what you are about to learn.

He gets on a roll, and you cannot shut him up! You know there is a storyline in what he is saying somewhere, but the words... the sentences... the paragraphs... the minutes... the hours... they all seem to run together.

You are going to learn how to be like a 6-year-old using...

Punctuation Ambiguity

The key to conversational hypnosis is creating a transderivational search... actually... a series of transderivational searches in your subject.

One way, and a very good way, is what you have been learning... ambiguities.

Punctuation ambiguity is so subtle, and it has a very large impact.

So, what is it?

Punctuation ambiguity occurs when you put two sentences together in the following way...

The last word of sentence #1 is also the first word of sentence #2.

Let me give you an example...

"Tom, we've talked about several ways that I can help your sales staff increase their income. I get the feeling that you understand that this is a large <u>benefit</u> now by moving forward with this training."

Did you catch the **punctuation ambiguity**?

"Benefit" in the above example is called a **pivot word**. In this instance, "benefit" has two meanings, both as a noun and a verb; and it can belong to either of the two sentences...

- "I get the feeling that you understand that this is a large <u>benefit</u>."
- "<u>Benefit</u> now by moving forward with this training."

Notice how there is no period separating the two sentences in the example.

Your mind must enter a transderivational search in order to give meaning to the two sentences.

What surprised me the most when I first learned and began to use **punctuation ambiguities** years ago was the fact that I **never** got caught. No one ever noticed them, and they would **always** accept the suggestion.

Start by practicing in a "safe" environment, such as the family dinner table. Perhaps you could say...

"On the way home today, a moving van's door flew open; and this car was about hit with a very big piece of wood you pass the salt please?"

In this example, note that the word "wood" is also a phonological ambiguity. In other words, "wood" and "would" sound the same.

You will find that no one will question, or even catch, what you just said; and they will pass the salt.

Watch for the brief transderivational search as you execute the **punctuation ambiguity**. Artfully woven throughout a conversation, **punctuation ambiguities** will direct your subject's mind and install suggestions very quickly.

Let's take a few more examples to help you get a grasp on **punctuation ambiguities**...

- "You'll find that you can learn conversational hypnosis faster as you learn to keep your mind open up to new possibilities."
- "When you take a look at my references and experience, you'll discover that I do very thorough work me into your training plans."

145

- "Earlier this evening, some stranger walked up to take my picture you and me having a very good time. I was a little surprised when she asked. You know what I mean?"
- "I wonder if you can pay attention to your hand me the glass."
- "Have you ever let your imagination run away with you can write your number right here."
- "Last night, I was out late at the grocery store this information deep inside your mind."

Get the idea?

The easiest way to learn, develop, and use **punctuation ambiguities** is to plan them out before you need them.

Write down the suggestions that you want to give, develop a sentence that ends in the word that your suggestion begins with, and put them together.

What are your meta programs?

What are your **meta programs**?

Who cares?!?

Well, you should know your own, but you also need to know your subject's.

So, what are **meta programs**?

Meta programs are general, habitual patterns that are commonly used by a person across a wide range of situations. In other words, **meta programs** are the habits that people unconsciously follow when making decisions and communicating.

By learning the most common **meta programs** of your subject, you will enter their world and influence them very powerfully.

Let's go through the <u>six</u> most common **meta programs**...

1

Direction Sort - Does your subject tend to "move toward" or "move away"?

To find out, ask a question such as...

"What do you want in a relationship?"... and listen to the response. The actual answer is not as important as **how** the answer is stated.

If your subject answers by saying, "Well, I don't want what I had in my last relationship; and I don't want someone who doesn't listen to me."

This answer indicates that this person has "moving away" as a direction sort. They are listing things that they do not want.

If, on the other hand, your subject answers by saying, "I want someone who I can wake up with and feel grateful. I want to find someone who I can be happy with for the rest of my life."

This answer indicates that this person has "moving toward" as a direction sort. They are listing things that they want in a relationship.

When you learn this information, how do you use it?

You speak to your subject in the language that they need to hear...

Moving Toward... "Tammy, if you go out with me, I promise that you'll have a great time. We can see how many things we have in common. What do you say?"

Moving Away... "Tammy, if you pass up the chance to see how much we have in common, you may be making a big mistake and miss your chance at a great relationship. Let's meet for coffee."

Most likely, one of these statements seems almost "rude" or too "wishy washy" to you. It is because it is not your normal meta program.

It is not rude, it is simply how your subject needs to hear it. **Stay out of your head, and enter your subject's.**

2
Reason Sort - Is it possibility or necessity?

In order to influence someone, it is important to determine if your subject is operating out of possibility or necessity.

This will not only help you decide in which direction to take the conversation, but it also allows you to speak their language.

To find out if your subject is operating out of possibility or necessity, ask a question such as... "Why did you choose your present job?"

If your subject answers by saying, "I saw a chance for upward mobility, and that is what I want"; then your subject is operating out of possibility.

If your subject answers by saying, "I could not find anything else. The job market was down, and I needed to be making money"; then your subject is operating out of necessity.

Keep in mind that the questions you ask will be related to your conversation. For example, if you are talking about your subject's relationship problems, then you might ask... "Why did you begin dating your girlfriend?"

If, on the other hand, you are a salesperson selling a copying machine, you might ask... "Why did you choose the copier that you have now?"

After finding out how your subject operates, speak to them in their language. For example, if you are encouraging a friend to take a new job, you could say...

Possibility... "Think of the impact you could make on so many people by taking this new job. You could really make a difference!"

Necessity... "You need to take this job if you want to make an impact on people's lives. To make a real difference, you have to be in this position."

Notice the same theme, but it is a different way of saying it.

Go out and practice these first two **meta programs**. Begin to pay attention to how people say things as well as what people are saying. Discover their Direction and Reason Sorts, and speak to them in their language.

On the next lesson, we will add to your awareness of

meta programs to focus your communication even further.

Until then, you will already begin to notice an increase in your ability to influence by using just these first two **meta programs**.

Let's do some more programming.

In your last lesson, you learned about two **meta programs**:

- Direction Sort
- Reason Sort

Just by recognizing and using these two **meta programs**, your influence over others will skyrocket.

In this lesson, I am going to introduce you to two more **meta programs**. It is your responsibility to master this material. Learn it, practice it, and own it.

3
Frame Of Reference - Does your subject have an "internal" or "external" frame of reference?

In other words, does your subject march to the beat of their own drum, or does your subject need reassurance from others?

How do you discover from which frame of reference your subject is currently operating? I suggest asking a question such as this...

"How do you know when you have done a great job?"

If you get the response, "I just know that I have done a great job"; then your subject is operating out of an internal frame of reference.

If you get the response, "When people say something positive about what I have done either to me or to someone else"; then your subject is operating out of an external frame of reference.

After discovering from what frame of reference your subject is operating, then use it to influence them.

If your subject is operating from an internal frame of reference, say things like, "I don't know what is right for you in this area. I'm sure you know deep down. What do you think about it?"

If your subject is operating from an external frame of reference, say things like, "Do this, because Tom did it and loved it and Jenny cannot stop talking about it; and it can work for you as well."

4
Attention Sort - Is your subject more focused on themselves (self) or on others (other)?

This is one of the easiest **meta programs** to recognize. All you have to do is **watch**! You watch, because like the other **meta programs**, attention sort happens outside of your subject's awareness.

Let's discuss both <u>self</u> and <u>other</u>.

<u>Self</u>... Your subject is focused on their **own** perceptions, values, beliefs, et cetera. <u>Self</u> is related to both confidence and assertiveness (healthy) and behaviors of a sociopath (destructive).

<u>Other</u>... Your subject is focused on **other people's** perceptions, values, beliefs, et cetera. <u>Other</u> is related to both compassion and caring (healthy) and behaviors of co-dependence (destructive).

A major airline currently incorporates **attention sort** in their hiring process.

Part of the hiring process for flight attendants is to prepare a 3-minute presentation about themselves that will be given to a room full of other applicants... and this is a very large audience.

The applicants believe that they are being judged on their presentation and speaking skills as well as their feelings of comfort in front of a group of people.

NO! That is not what is being judged!

The company is watching the **<u>audience members</u>**. They are watching to see which audience members are **focused on the presenter** in the front of the room and not on going over their own material.

Why?

Because the airline wants their flight attendants to watch and attend to the needs of the passengers... not themselves.

What types of people do you want in different areas of your life? Attention sort allows you to quickly discover if your subject is someone you would like to spend a lot of time with or run the other way instead.

I have posted the checklist that I use with my coaching clients when determining from which **meta programs** a client is operating. You can view this checklist online and download it for your own reference.

You will see that there are a couple of other meta programs on the checklist that we have not talked about yet. Remember when we started the lessons on meta programs, I said that I would teach you six. We are only on number four! The other two will be in your next lesson.

To view and download my **Meta Programs Checklist**, go to… https://bit.ly/3dWyVZ3

Your third and final lesson on meta programs.

So, now you know about...

- Direction Sort,
- Reason Sort,
- Frame Of Reference, and
- Attention Sort.

There are two other **meta programs** that you should know and use...

5
Relationship Sort - Is your subject a matcher or mismatcher?

People tend to see the <u>sameness</u> in things or the <u>differences</u> in things.

For example, if I put a nickel, a dime, and a quarter on the table; what is the relationship?

Some people will say that they are all coins. Those

people would be <u>matchers</u>.

Others would say that they are all different amounts. Those people would be <u>mismatchers</u>.

In a normal conversation, simply asking what the relationship of _____ is will give you a good idea of your subject's **relationship sort**.

Some people can be a <u>combination</u>... "Well, they're all coins, but they're different amounts."   OR   "Well, they're all different amounts, but they're all coins.

Listen for each of the four classifications...

- Sameness
- Difference
- Sameness with exception
- Difference with exception

After discovering your subject's preference, use it.

For example, suppose you are influencing a partner to begin a new project. All of these statements are referring to the exact same project, but they are talking to different **relationship sort** styles...

If you find that your subject is operating out of <u>sameness</u>; then you may say something like, "This is very similar to the project that we took on about a year ago, and it worked out very well. Let's go ahead and do this."

If you find that your subject is operating out of <u>difference</u>; then you may say something like, "This is something very different than anything we've ever done before, and it is an exciting time to take this sort of project on. Let's go ahead and do this."

If you find that your subject is operating out of sameness with exception; then you may say something like, "This is similar to the project that we took on about a year ago, but it is different in its design and purpose. Let's go ahead and do this."

If you find that your subject is operating out of difference with exception; then you may say something like, "This is something different than anything we've done before, but it looks to be a hit like our project about a year ago. Let's go ahead and do this."

6
Convincer - How is your subject convinced?

This is a very simple, yet very powerful, **meta program**. It has two parts.

Part number one, does your subject need to see someone do it, hear about someone doing it, actually do it with someone, or read about someone doing it?

For example, you could ask, "How do you know when someone is good at what he does?"

Does your subject need to see, hear, do, or read to determine if someone is good at what he does?

Part number two, how often does your subject need to be convinced?

Does your subject...

1. Immediately know that someone is good by just one demonstration?
2. Need a number of demonstrations (two or more) to know that someone is good?
3. Need a period of time (like two weeks, three months, a year) to know that someone is good?
4. Need consistent proof that someone is good?

This **meta program** gives you a plan for influencing your subject. You know in advance what has to be done to influence each person, and you keep from becoming frustrated with someone who consistently needs to be reminded.

You now have what I consider the six main **meta programs**.

Use them together to enter your subject's world, and communicate with your subject using their own meta programs.

Your influence over others will increase exponentially.

Give them "the look".

Have you ever gotten "the look" from someone... say a parent... and you knew that they meant business? You felt that certain feeling rush through your body, and you did not really have control over it.

You could chalk that feeling up to a simple "anchor", but I think it is much more than that; and it is something that you can learn to use yourself with anyone at any time.

Throwing Emotion is a unique skill to instantly induce a specific emotional state in your subject... no matter if your subject is a stranger or your best friend.

The steps are easy, but they must be carried out with complete and utter confidence in your ability.

Step 1
You go first!

You must completely experience the emotion that you want your subject to feel. Without personal power, this can be a scary thing for some people.

To do this, think about a time when you felt the particular emotion. See what you saw at the time, hear what you heard, and really feel the feeling.

Step 2

At the most intense point of your emotional state, turn to your subject, stare directly INTO their eyes, and imagine that you are transferring that state to them.

When you look into their eyes, you must focus your stare at a point approximately two inches behind the surface of their eyes... imagine you are looking into their soul and the deepest recesses of their mind. Think of it as almost looking through them.

But here is the real trick, and the coolest part — do not express any of your internal feelings externally. In other words, do not let your facial expression or body language give your feelings and intention away.

Continue your "stare" until you observe that your subject is experiencing the emotion that you would like them to experience. This is usually obvious by their body language, breathing rate, how they speak, et cetera.

The real beauty of this technique is that your subject will feel the shift toward the target emotion without a clue that it is coming from YOU.

This is really just the same as when one individual can get a whole group of people to freak out simply by getting very agitated and upset about something. The negative feelings simply transfer to others. In that kind of situation, the origin of the feeling is obvious.

With "the look", you are being covert about inducing the emotion.

Step 3

As soon as your subject is experiencing the intended emotion, you may stay in the same emotion as they are and have a great time; or you can instantly change your emotional state to accomplish your specific goal.

For example, perhaps you transferred a wanton buying state to your subject. As soon as your subject takes on the state, you can then instantly switch to a persuasive state to finish your sales pitch.

Want another example?... Let's say you are approached while in a bar by a patron simply wanting to cause problems. You can transfer an intense sense of fear and intimidation to this person. As soon as you notice that your subject has taken on the fear and intimidation, instantly put yourself into a very confident state. You can now handle the situation.

This may seem a little far-fetched, but is actually quite easy once you know the trick and practice beforehand.

To quickly change states, you will utilize anchoring. You already know how to do this.

Sound way out there for you? Practice and use this technique for a week. You will find that it is very effective.

BONUS: Install suggestions directly into your subject's unconscious mind.

This bonus lesson was added several years after the first release of the book you are reading. It is a critical skill that can make a world of difference if you take the time to master it.

I recently held a boot camp in which I taught **nested loops**. Afterward, a student came up to me and asked why I had not included nested loops in this book. I answered that I just hadn't gotten to them yet. The real answer... I did not know how to make the concept clear enough in written form.

After much thought, my hope is that this explanation is clear enough that you can take this very powerful method of **unconscious installation** and use It... now.

Unconscious installation is presenting suggestions and information to people of which they are unaware but carry out nevertheless.

The reason that I always viewed nested loops as difficult to teach is the careful planning that is needed as you begin to learn how to communicate in this way. Even in my live boot camps, students will understand it in class; but they will not put in the time to master the skill when they leave the boot camp. I urge you to really put some time into this. The benefits you will have for the rest of your life will far outweigh the small amount of time you spend mastering nested loops now.

Remember from previous lessons how the unconscious mind is compelled to make sense of all the information it receives?

Think of transderivational searches... your unconscious mind **needs** to add meaning to what you are experiencing.

Furthermore, your unconscious has a need to close any unfinished idea or experience (or loop), and it is able to follow many loops at any one time.

Creating a loop is very easy, because it is nothing more than storytelling. Are you a good story teller?

Let's see...

1. Do you capture your listener's attention? If you do not, the loop is closed right then and there. When you lose your listener's attention, their mind has shut down. **You must capture their attention**.

2. Can you "move" people emotionally? Nested loops can connect emotional states. By connecting these emotional states, you can lead people in the direction that you choose. Your goal is to direct your listener's thoughts.

3. And most important of all... You embed information and suggestions inside these stories (loops). When each story (loop) is closed (completed), the information and suggestions collapse into your listener's unconscious. This creates amnesia, and your listener is completely unaware that any sort of installation process has taken place.

Nested loops are complex, and they use multiple stories. Each story is interrupted part of the way through, and the next story begins. If you have been in any of my boot camps, then you may or may not have been aware that I am always doing this.

How would you know that this is happening to you? Well, many people become increasingly curious and sometimes a bit frustrated at the same time, because it is difficult to keep track of the stories and they do not know how some of the stories end... yet.

Emotions, information, and suggestions are embedded in the stories (loops) during the process as each story (loop) is closed in reverse order.

Let me explain the structure a little better...

1. Start story 1 (Evoke an emotional state with your story that you want your listener to feel.)

2. Interrupt story 1, and begin story 2 (Evoke another emotional state with your story that you want your listener to feel.)
3. Interrupt story 2, and begin story 3 (Evoke yet another emotional state with your story that you want your listener to feel.)
4. Continue interrupting and beginning as many stories as you would like.
5. When you get to your last story, you tell the story fully as you embed information and suggestions. Then, go on to the next step.
6. Complete your stories in reverse order. For example, if you have a total of three stories that you started, then you finish story 3 then story 2 then story 1.

My boot camps (and nearly every one of my interactions with anyone) use several nested loops.

Keep in mind that loops can be closed in the same conversation, the same hour, the same day, or weeks or months later.

Here is your homework...

1. Write down five pieces of information and suggestions you want to install in your listener. (Examples... buy now, make a change, you like this idea, et cetera)
2. Write down five emotional states that you would like to elicit in your listener. (Examples... curiosity, intrigue, desire, et cetera)
3. Write out five stories. These stories can be real life happenings or they can be stories that you create. Each of these stories should

illustrate one of your five emotional states. For example, perhaps you tell a story of a time that you were really curious about something. As you tell the story, your goal is to get your listener to feel the curiosity that you are describing. (NOTE: If you have five emotional states, you will have five stories... a story for each emotional state that you want to elicit.)

4. In the middle of each story, you will jump to the next story. Determine where and how you will interrupt each story and how you will jump to the next story. (You may use phrases like "That reminds me of another time..." or "It is like the time I..." or "Remember when you were younger...".) In other words, you are only telling half of each story before starting the next one.

5. When you get to your last story, you will tell this story in its entirety. This is also the story in which you give the pieces of information and suggestions you want to install in your listener. Be very direct. For example, "After jumping out of that tree, I realized, Dave, something must change." (NOTE: In this example, I want to install "something must change". I purposely say the listener's name immediately before the suggestion "something must change" so that Dave's unconscious knows that I am talking to him.) Use this format in this last story for each of the pieces of information and suggestions you have to install. Now, complete this last story.

6. Proceed to complete all of the remaining stories IN REVERSE ORDER.

7.   Your listener will tend to develop amnesia for the last story (the middle story of the loop process), but the pieces of information and suggestions will still be carried out by their unconscious mind.
8.   Practice, practice, practice.

This is one of the most powerful methods of covertly installing ideas, information, suggestions, et cetera into the unconscious minds of others. This skill is a must to master if you truly want to become an expert communicator and leader.

If you are still a bit confused, consider attending one of my boot camps. You will truly leave a different person.

For information contact...

Bill Gladwell

(702) 721-8456

HypnosisForHumans.com
Bill@HypnosisForHumans.com

Printed in Great Britain
by Amazon